David Adam was born in Alnwick, Northumberland. He was Vicar of Danby on the North Yorkshire Moors for over twenty years, where he discovered the gift for writing prayers in the Celtic pattern. His first book of these, *The Edge of Glory*, achieved immediate popularity. He has since published several collections of prayers and meditations based on the Celtic tradition and the lives of the Celtic saints. His books have been translated into various languages, including Finnish and German, and have appeared in American editions. Many of his prayers have now been set to music. After thirteen years as Vicar of Holy Island, where he had taken many retreats and regularly taught school groups on prayer, David moved to Waren Mill in Northumberland from where he continues his work and writing.

THE HOLY ISLAND OF LINDISFARNE

DAVID ADAM

Illustrations by Monica Capoferri

Unless otherwise noted, scripture quotations are taken from the
New Revised Standard Version of the Bible, Anglicized Edition,
copyright © 1989, 1995 by the Division of Christian Education of
the National Council of the Churches of Christ in the USA.
Used by permission. All rights reserved.

First published in Great Britain in 2009 by
Society for Promoting Christian Knowledge, 36 Causton Street,
London SW1P 4ST

First published in North America in 2009 by
Morehouse Publishing, 4775 Linglestown Road, Harrisburg, PA 17112
Morehouse Publishing, 445 Fifth Avenue, New York, NY 10016

Morehouse Publishing is an imprint of Church Publishing Incorporated.

Illustrations copyright © Monica Capoferri 2009
Taliesin poems are translated by Meirion Pennar and published by
Llanerch Press Ltd. Extract from *The Anglo-Saxon World* by
Kevin Crossley-Holland, published by Boydell & Brewer,
is reproduced with permission.

Library of Congress Cataloging-in-Publication Data

A catalog record of this book is available from the Library of Congress

ISBN: 978-0-8192-2344-9

Typeset by Graphicraft Ltd, Hong Kong
Printed in the UK by CPI Bookmarque, Croydon, CR0 4TD
Produced on paper from sustainable forests

09 10 11 12 13 14   10 9 8 7 6 5 4 3 2 1

Contents

A Now and Then Island   1

The Case of the Severed Head   9

Aidan and the Handing on of the Light   19

The Keys of the Kingdom   35

Cuthbert Afire with Love   47

The Golden Age of Northumbria   61

The Fury of the Norsemen   69

Island Church and Priory   77

The Castle and Some Characters   87

Both God and the Devil   101

Timeline   112

Glossary   115

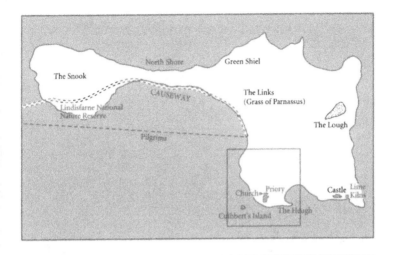

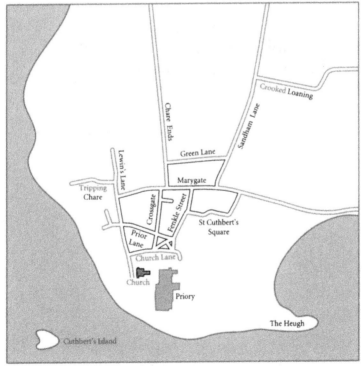

The Holy Island of Lindisfarne, showing inset detail.

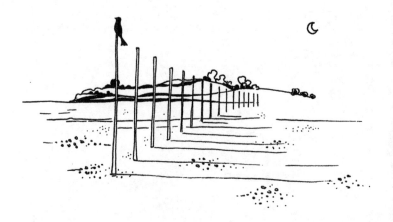

A Now and Then Island

For, with the flow and ebb its stile
Varies from continent to isle;
Dry-shod, o'er sands, twice every day,
The pilgrims to the shrine find way:
Twice every day, the waves efface
Of staves and sandaled feet the trace.
(Walter Scott, *Marmion: A Tale of
Flodden Field*, II.9, London,
Cassell, 1904, pp. 39–40)

As a young child in the early 1940s, I often passed Lindisfarne when we took the train up to Dundee to stay with my grandparents. Set in a silver sea, its fairy-tale castle rising up to touch the sky, I imagined it must be an extraordinary place, a place of mystery.

In fact, my first visit to the island was in a lorry loaded with concrete pipes! My father and I had often driven past Lindisfarne in his NAAFI van during the last years of the Second World War, and he had told me that Aidan and Cuthbert lived there. At first I was uncertain if he was talking of now or long ago; it was not until much later that I began to learn how the past often vibrates in the present.

This particular day he thought would be a good opportunity for me to see the island. We waited – in growing anticipation on my side – as the tide went out. There was no metalled road then, and driving all the way across the sands was exciting in itself. Bamburgh castle stood majestically down to the south; the Cheviot hills with their frosting of snow were behind me, and we passed a wealth of birds, including more ducks and geese than I had ever seen before in my life. The wooden poles, sunk into the seabed to mark a safe crossing, gave a wonderful sense of perspective as they disappeared into the distance. When we arrived on the island proper, I felt I had travelled to another land. Somehow, though it looked much like the countryside we'd left behind, the island seemed not of the same world as the rest of England. Perhaps this was the very thing that attracted St Aidan and his monks: here the Other does not invade, but rather pervades, at every turn – for those who have eyes to see.

While my father encouraged me to think of the island as a place of story, romance and adventure, my uncle Jackie's view was rather more down to earth. He delivered coal there; for him it was a place of work, and tough in many ways. He related how local football teams were afraid of playing against the islanders because there was always the danger, if the visiting team won, that the islanders would throw them into the sea!

———◆◆◆———

Of course, Lindisfarne is only a now and then island, governed by the moon and the tides. When I was its vicar, a child would often approach me with a most difficult question, 'Where is Holy Island?' Though she was standing on it and had walked around it, the answer was not simple because at that moment it was not an island at all! The truth is that for most daily pilgrims their journey's end is a village built on the far reaches of the mainland. They have not crossed any sea, but only driven along the road or walked the Pilgrim's Causeway.

But twice a day, for two spells of five hours, Lindisfarne is completely cut off and the only way you can get to it is by boat from Seahouses. Then it takes on a stillness and a brightness that can almost be felt, with the sea all around increasing the amount of light through reflection. The Venerable Bede (*c.* 673–753), who was interested in the tides and their relationship to the phases of the moon, said of Lindisfarne:

2

> As the tide ebbs and flows, this place is surrounded by sea twice
> a day like an island, and twice a day the sand dries and joins it
> to the mainland.
>
> (Bede, *A History of the English Church and People*,
> Book III:3, trans. Leo Sherley-Price, Penguin,
> 1968, p. 145; hereafter, Bede, *A History*)

Later in the ninth century Aethelwulf, a monk of the Cuthbert
folk, living at Crayke near York, mentions the tide change over
the island:

> ... where the waves are eager to curl over the shores with grey
> water: but rush to lay them bare as they go to their backward
> course, and the blue depths encircle a sacred land, and afford a
> ready journey when they lay the shores bare.

Those who live on Lindisfarne, and those who visit, soon
realize that the sands are not covered by only a negligible
amount of water at high tide. It is the North Sea that floods in!
It comes not with a mighty rush, but in a manner that ensures
you cannot then drive on or off the island at all. There are
plenty of notices and warnings concerning the danger, yet every
year many have to be rescued from their cars by lifeboat from
Seahouses or by helicopter from nearby RAF Boulmer. Sometimes cars can be completely submerged at high tide and suffer
serious damage, at least to their electrical works and interior.
Driving to the island late one night, I saw a 4x4 that had been
swept off the causeway in the dark and it was buried up to its
axles in sand. Fortunately the occupants made it safely to the
island. It cannot be emphasized enough that all visitors must
pay high regard to the tide and check times carefully, for these
change every day of the year.

In the registers belonging to the parish church, there are
several accounts of people being caught by the tide and losing
their lives:

Jan 8th 1584, old John Stapleton drowned
Nov 5th 1641 Samuel Waddell and his son drowned in the Low

A Now and Then Island

July 28th 1746 Rob Brown, Clerk of Holy Island drowned
April 8th 1801 William Macmillan drowned in passing the
sands
Dec 15th 1802 Alexander Warwick drowned in crossing the
sands.

———◆———

There is no doubt the island is an attractive place visually, spiritually and romantically. It is full of surprises and contrasts: a place of peace where there have also been battles and slaughter; a place of holiness and sanctuary that has been invaded more than once and well-nigh destroyed; a place with a small population that hosts almost half a million visitors a year. But though thousands visit each day in the summer, there are still great stretches of silence and emptiness. The expanse of beaches, the sky and the seascapes take the breath away, and fill any feeling person with awe. When the island is at its busiest, you can still escape to the Grass of Parnassus and hear the larks sing as they rise on the air. You can walk among the meadow orchids and northern marsh orchids and listen to the curlew's call, or look across an expanse of thrift and hear the common seals singing on the sandbanks. On a misty morning, this can be a wonderful, eerie experience!

The Lindisfarne National Nature Reserve, of which Holy Island is a central part, covers around eight thousand acres – from Goswick Sands in the north, down to where I now live, at Budle Bay in the south. The sands, mudflats, dunes, salt marsh and estuary of the River Low are a delight to the botanist, the explorer and, of course, the birdwatcher. The island itself is the first landfall after the North Sea for many migrating birds: I have seen the streets filled with tiny goldcrests exhausted after travelling from Scandinavia, and, on another occasion, the wonderful spectacle of nine short-eared owls circling together on a sunny January afternoon.

On the Reserve, wildfowl and waders over-winter in great flocks. Almost all the two thousand pale-bellied Brent Geese from the Spitsbergen breeding grounds in Norway stay on the mudflats, though they are outnumbered by wigeon, whose numbers were as high as 19,955 in October 2002. Waders in winter include knot, dunlin, bar-tailed godwit, curlew and oystercatcher in abundance. The bird many most like to see, though, is the eider duck because of its association with St Cuthbert (of which more later).

The island is not large, and it is easy to cover its eight-mile perimeter in a day. From quite a few vantage points, it is possible to see the sun rise and set in the sea, and there are not many places in Britain you can do that! Having looked down on the island from the air, once in a Tiger Moth and once in a helicopter, I have seen for myself that it is shaped like an axe. Legend has it that when Satan made war in heaven, his battle axe was struck from his hand, fell to earth and landed in the sea, becoming the island of Lindisfarne. The head of the axe is about a mile square, and along its sharp edge lies most of the village, with names like Fiddler's Green, Crooked Loaning, Tripping Chare, St Cuthbert's Square and Fenkle Street telling of its past. (For many years, the profile of the island reminded me of something else, and one day, when I opened a favourite book of mine, *The Little Prince* by Antoine de Saint-Exupéry, I realized it was the Little Prince's picture of a boa constrictor digesting an elephant that his grown-up audience mistook for a drawing of a hat! Look at the castle in its position on rugged Beblow Crag, and you will see why!)

Walking round the island you will discover upturned herring boats used for sheds, sandy lanes with wind-blasted hawthorns, and sand dunes where it is possible to see the remains of an early medieval farming settlement. The lovely freshwater lake, the Lough, has a hide which offers wonderful birdwatching: the flight of starlings in their thousands to the reeds of the Lough on autumn evenings is a sight not to be missed. Not far away, on the edge of the island, is a stone pyramid painted white, which acts as a warning guide to shipping – the island has some low-lying cliffs and two outcrops of the Great Whin Sill, which stretches right across Northumberland. Dolerite rock has thrust its way through the limestone to create Beblow Crag, on which the castle stands sentinel over the harbour, and the Heugh, from where you get a wonderful panoramic view of the Farne Islands out at sea, Bamburgh castle to the south, the Cheviots to the west, and the towns of Berwick-on-Tweed, and St Abbs Head (over the border in Scotland) to the north. Just below the Heugh on the landward side lie the ruins of the Norman priory, the Church of St Mary the Virgin, and the vicarage. Just west of the vicarage is the little tidal island known as Cuthbert's Island.

———————◆———————

Before the last glacial period of the current ice age (yes, technically we are still in one!), when England was linked to Europe by a land bridge, the Lindisfarne section of the coast was probably about four miles out from its present position. However, when the ice began to melt and sea levels to rise, Britain and Lindisfarne became islands. During this time, nomadic hunter-gatherers followed vast herds of deer, akin to the giant Irish elk, which were perhaps a million strong. These deer could have an antler span of around 15 feet and when caught would supply up to nearly 1 ton of meat. Excavations at nearby Howick have revealed the site of a house occupied by such hunters for a period of over three hundred years: its position, near the estuary stream and the sea, shows they knew how to supplement their diet with the harvest of stream and sea. In fact, nomadic hunter-gatherers seem to have occupied much of the south-east coast of Scotland. There is evidence they made effective spears by the process of embedding a series of specially shaped flint blades in grooves in a length of bone, and using beech bark resin as an adhesive. Flint tools and flints used in food preparation, such as cutters and scrapers, have been found in considerable quantities on Lindisfarne, including mesolithic (middle Stone Age) microliths, and the leaf shaped and tanged arrow heads of the neolithic ('new' Stone Age) and Bronze Age. I know of one woman on the island who treasures a neolithic polished stone axe head she dug out of her garden. In the grounds of the vicarage, various finds from the Bronze Age and each era up to the present have been discovered.

The history of Lindisfarne feels to me like the history of England in miniature, and the rest of this book tells the island's vibrant story from the sixth century up to the present day. This tiny place was the setting of one of the last stands of the 'British' – the Celtic peoples who occupied most of Britain before the English, otherwise known as the Anglo-Saxons (an assortment of Germanic peoples). The island has been the home of saints and scholars. It saw the making, in the late seventh or early eighth century, of one of our greatest artistic and religious treasures, the Lindisfarne Gospels. It experienced the first recorded Viking invasion in 793. It has one of the best preserved early medieval farm settlements. Its eleventh-century priory and sixteenth-century castle still draw pilgrims and visitors from all over the world. The island was involved in the seventeenth-century Civil War, and the eighteenth-century Jacobite Rebellion, and signs of the burgeoning Industrial Revolution may be found too.

Wherever you walk on Lindisfarne, the past impinges on the present. The island's legends and stories are very much alive, and you may well suddenly feel that you have left the now and entered an age hidden away . . . just beneath the surface.

The Case of the Severed Head

A head I bear by the side of my thigh,
That was the shield of his country,
That was a wheel in battle,
That was a ready sword in his country's battles
A head that I bear on my sword . . .
In Aber Lleu* has Urien been slain.

> (sixth-century poem attributed to Llywarch
> Hen in William F. Skene, *Four Ancient
> Books of Wales*, Edinburgh, 1868)

*Aber Lleu is thought to be the Ross Sands (on Lindisfarne) where the River Low runs into the sea.

The year was 1993. It had been a strange morning. I had taken a phone call from the Dean of Trondheim Cathedral in Norway, who told me that a group of Norwegians were keen to make a pilgrimage to the island in penitence for the Viking invasion of 793. Sorrow being expressed for an event now more than twelve hundred years old! It is amazing how race memory seems to be at work in our times. This visit, however, would strengthen the growing bonds between the Norwegian church and the diocese of Newcastle. After we had amiably discussed various things the visitors might do on Holy Island, the Dean's final remark came as a bit of a shock: 'We would like to present you with St Olaf's Head.' What could I say? I had a vision of myself as a present-day Hamlet, meditating, 'Alas, poor Olaf!' Only later did I realize I was being offered not this wonderful relic, but a copy of a stone carving of St Olaf's head from the cathedral. It came as quite a relief.

The causeway was about to open, but there was time for a quick walk before the daily invasion of pilgrims. I stood on the Heugh, the highest point on Holy Island, and gazed southwards through a light mist towards the beacons on Ross Sands. These two strange-looking pinnacles, rather like Cleopatra's Needles, guide boats into Holy Island harbour and have to be seen in line for entry to be safe. Near the pinnacles, on the lonely stretches of Ross Sands, terns make their nests in places that appear to be out of harm's way. It all looks quite idyllic, but at this moment I am watching a kestrel searching for an easy meal. This little colony of terns is being decimated by predators – kestrel, crow and fox – and on my last visit I had seen three decapitated adult birds. As I continued gazing this misty morning, I noticed a man beyond the pinnacles carrying something in his right hand. It may have been a bag of winkles, but with my mind still full of poor Olaf, my thoughts immediately went to the first ever recorded event on Lindisfarne: the case of the severed head.

Somewhere by the Ross pinnacles lies the body of a long-forgotten British king.

———◆———

In the late sixth century, the warlord Urien ruled a kingdom known as Rheged. It stretched down the west coast, from Galloway to the estuary of the Dee, and across towards the east, through the Yorkshire Dales possibly as far as Catterick: the poet Taliesin says Urien was 'lord of Catterick'. It is largely because Taliesin's songs about Urien survived long enough to be committed to writing in thirteenth-century Wales – in the 'Canu Taliesin' or 'Book of Taliesin' – that we know Urien's story at all. He is remembered as a heroic figure, who sought to unite the British against the invading English.

Those who lived in Urien's hill-fort stronghold were a cultured people, with a highly developed sense of art and beauty: here you would find exquisite clothing, mead, beer, wine, and gold work of a most intricate and artistic standard. Urien's warriors were great horsemen, the horse being regarded as a symbol of their power and wealth. The leaders of these men underlined their position and authority by wearing torques of gold when all rode out to battle; round shields, shining blue armour and throwing spears would also be on show. A leader who was victorious in battle would show his generosity by sharing out any spoils with his men, and a strong leader like Urien was a good man to follow.

He was certainly given great support by the poet Taliesin. In the upbeat song, 'The Battle of Wensleydale', Taliesin tells of a victorious battle in which Urien-ap-Rheged is described as a 'king of the baptised world' – in other words, a Christian fighting the pagan English, and making a stand, for his land and for his faith. Though, notice Urien is also described as a cattle rustler!

> The men of Catraeth,
> at the break of dawn,
> arise,
> around your triumphant rustler-king.
> For this is Urien,
> famous leader.
> He keeps his chiefs at bay
> and scythes them down.
> Warlike daimon has he,
> In truth the king of the baptised world,
> The scourge of the men of Britain
> In their battle lines . . .
> (*Taliesin Poems*, trans. Meiron Pennar,
> Llanerch, 1988, p. 51)

'The Battle of Wensleydale' was composed when the British appeared to have the upper hand against the English. Though the invaders had taken the coastal area, the Britons seemed to be unconquered further inland, and Taliesin was sure that with such a strong leader, the northern British could drive the English out. This song would be sung by the warriors around the campfires and as they travelled:

If there's an enemy on the hill,
Urien will make him shudder.
If there is an enemy in the hollow,
Urien will pierce him through.
If there is an enemy on the mountain,
Urien will bruise him.
If there's an enemy on the dyke,
Urien will strike him down.
> (*Taliesin Poems*, p. 70)

In another of his battle poems, Taliesin tells of a victory against Fflamddwyn, 'the Flame Bearer', whose title probably describes a scorched earth approach to destroying villages and communities. In this battle Urien and his son Owain share the victory, though Taliesin shows some of the posturing of the leaders. The Flame Bearer mockingly calls, 'Have my hostages come?', to which Owain replies, 'They have not come because they do not exist.' There was no way Urien's men would be demoralized or defeated by the Flame Bearer: rather, they would triumph, and send these incomers either back to where they belonged, or to their death. Indeed, we are told in another song that Owain killed the Flame Bearer.

In the poem entitled 'You are the Best', Taliesin reminds us again that Urien was part of a Christian society and suggests that he is well able to keep the English at bay:

Urien of Erechwydd,
Christendom's most generous man,
a myriad of gifts
you give
to the men of the world.
As you hoard
you scatter.
While your life lasts
the poets of Christendom
are happy.
There is more joy
from having

one bounteous, famous.
There is more glory around
because Urien and his sons exist.
And he's the foremost of them –
an exalted chief-king,
a remote fortress,
a swift champion.
The English know of him
when they tell,
for at his hands
death
was dealt to them . . .
. . . The Angles are without protection
because of the most courageous lord.
(*Taliesin Poems*, pp. 57–8)

Taliesin paints a picture of a generous king who welcomes people to his royal hall, where there is drinking and feasting and the sharing of spoils gained from triumphs over the defeated English. It appears to be idyllic, but there are great clouds gathering. The poet Taliesin expresses worry that Urien, who is such a charismatic leader, is getting older. What will happen when the white-haired warrior does not return from one of his battles? If the British lose him, their head, how will the rest of the body fare?

Many years earlier, when Urien was still a youngster, plague had decimated the land, and the English had used this as an opportunity to come north and take over the stronghold of Bamburgh. It would seem another group now held a stronghold on Inis Metcaud, the oldest name for Lindisfarne, and Hussa, one of the descendants of Ida (the sixth-century ruler of the northern Northumbrian kingdom of Bernicia), was in control. The English were building up their strength and battle power, and if the British did not attack the coastal strongholds, the invaders would overrun the land. Under Urien's acknowledged leadership, Rhydderch the Old, who ruled the kingdom of Strathclyde from the fortress on Dumbarton Rock, rode with his warriors from the north; Gwallawg, the ruler of the kingdom of Elmet (around Leeds), came with his men from the south, while Urien's men arrived from the west, the three bands advancing on Bamburgh and Inis Metcaud in a pincer movement. Morcant, another northern British king, and his warriors were also part of this war band. With Urien at the helm, they felt assured of victory.

For three days and nights the British kept up their siege of the island and it would appear they could have won the day. The allegiance of the men of the North seemed to be strong enough and large enough to defeat the enemy, and if they had been successful we may never have become English! But there was an enemy within the ranks of the British, a leader who was jealous of the standing and power of Urien. Morcant turned traitor. On the third night of the siege, while the venerable warrior was asleep, Morcant crept over under the cover of darkness, drew his sword, and in one swift sweeping action beheaded him. He and his men fled the camp before dawn, and by the time the deed had been discovered, they were well away. The great army had lost its leader and the men of Rheged were anxious to leave for home, fearing Morcant would seek to appropriate some of their lands. And so the siege ended and the battle was lost. In the Welsh Triads, Morcant is called 'Llovan of the Severing Hand', and is remembered as the one who performed one of the 'Three Atrocious Assassinations of the Island of Britain'.

Though no poem by Taliesin recording this event has survived, 'The Head of Urien', which is attributed to Llywarch Hen, a cousin of the great leader, tells how he himself bore the head of Urien back to Rheged. Here are a few more lines from the poem that opened this chapter.

> A head I bear on my arm,
> He that overcame the land of Bryneich –
> But after being a hero, is now on a hearse.
> A head I bear in the grasps of my hand,

The Case of the Severed Head

> Of a chief that mildly governed the country;
> The head, the most powerful of Prydain . . .
> The delicate white corpse will be covered today;
> Under earth and blue stones . . .

Though Urien's head was carried off, the king's body was buried somewhere near where he fell. The description of blue stones well describes the colour of the dolerite found in this area.

Inis Metcaud saw one of the last stands of the Britons against the English in Northumbria. There would be one more major battle, at Catterick, a stronghold of Urien and his family, where the leader of the English, the heathen Aethelfrith, King of Northumbria, would prove to be a deadly foe. Between the siege of Inis Metcaud and the Battle of Catterick the English had increased in strength and fighting power, and Catterick had been captured and taken into Aethelfrith's possession.

Bede attributes to Aethelfrith an unparalleled fierceness:

> He ravaged the Britons more cruelly than all other English leaders, so that he might be compared to Saul the King of Israel, except of course he was ignorant of true religion. He overran a greater area than any other king or ealdorman, exterminating or enslaving the inhabitants making the lands either tributary to the English or ready for English settlement.
>
> (Bede, *A History*, p. 92)

The Catterick battle is remembered by yet another poet, Aneurin, in his sixth-century work 'The Gododdin'. The poem gives insights into the sort of men who opposed the English, young men who were Christian and went to their churches to do penance before the battle so that if they died, they died forgiven. The opening lines of the poem describe them:

> Of manly disposition was the youth,
> Valour had he in the tumult;
> Fleet thick-maned chargers
> Were under the thigh of the illustrious youth;
> A shield, light and broad

Was on the slender swift flank,
A sword blue and bright,
Golden spurs and ermine.

We are told the swords were 'blades full of vigour in defence of Baptism', and another verse, commenting on the death of Ceredig, 'an amiable leader', commends him to the Trinity:

May he find a complete reception
With the Trinity in perfect unity.

The Goddodin were known to the Romans as the Votadini and were from Edinburgh, Lothian and the Borders. Aneurin tells us how they were joined with other Britons from Rheged, Elmet, North Wales, Anglesey, Denbighshire, the area around Snowdon, Ayrshire, Bannog (around Stirling and Dumbarton), and from beyond the Firth of Forth. Yet for all this the British were decimated. Their strength as a fighting force in the north would not recover.

These battles remind us that Christianity was established in the north before the coming of Augustine to Canterbury in 597 or Aidan to Lindisfarne in the mid-seventh century. When Augustine summoned British bishops to a conference in 603, at least seven attended, as well as many learned men who came mainly from Bangor in North Wales. The British church was obviously well established and had its own centres of learning. In 616 at Chester, Aethelfrith put to death about twelve hundred monks who were mainly from Bangor because they were praying for the victory of the British. Bede tells us that Bangor alone had over two thousand monks, a hint of the strength of British Christianity. Bede complains that the British did not seek to convert the English but it is very hard to convert those who are set on killing the leaders of the community, including the monks and priests!

The failure of the British at the battle of Inis Metcaud looked like the beginning of darkness for the Christian faith in the North. But within half a century the flame would be rekindled on this small island, and a light would blaze out to illuminate the 'Dark Ages' and bring in the Golden Age of Northumbria.

———◆———

I had to leave the Heugh and return to the business of the day: there was a pilgrim group of five hundred coming in eight bus loads to hear how the island was the base for the growth of Christian mission and outreach. I wondered if they knew that Aidan was not the first Christian in the area, or that it has not always been a place of peace and tranquillity.

Aidan and the Handing on of the Light

And I said to the man who stood at the gate of the year:
'Give me a light that I may tread safely into the unknown.'
And he replied:
'Go out into the darkness
and put your hand into the Hand of God.
That shall be to you better than a light and safer than a
known way.'
(From Minnie Louise Hoskins' poem 'The Gate of the
Year' in *The Desert* (1908), quoted by King George VI
in his Christmas Broadcast, 1939)

Some days, when the mist lies low over its fairy-tale castle and romantic ruins, Lindisfarne still looks like the dream island of my childhood. And the light, when it breaks through the east window of the church in the very early morning, has a radiance that is almost palpable. As a Northumbrian born and bred, I have long been captivated by the beauty, wonder and holiness of this place. But when I was called to be vicar of Holy Island, I realized I would soon discover just how much of the dream you could actually live!

During the service in which I was inducted to the parish, I was given the key to the church, a stole embroidered with the figures of Aidan and Cuthbert, and a copy of the Lindisfarne Gospels. These signs of my inheritance represented a history of more than thirteen hundred years and reminded me of the great responsibility I faced. This little island has long been regarded not only as a special place but, as Rabbi Lionel Blue put it, the 'holiest place in holy England'. It certainly seems to have more saints per square metre than you can find almost anywhere else.

19

At the back of the church, before my first Sunday service, I looked at the list of bishops, priors, priests and incumbents who had been given pastoral care of the island. It began with Aidan in 635 and contained no fewer than sixteen bishops, including Finan, Colman, Eadfrith and Cuthbert. To follow such men (I spotted my name at the very bottom of the list!), and try to reflect something of their holiness, was a truly awesome challenge. A little consolation came with the knowledge that, like the sea, places and people ebb and flow: certainly, at times, the island has been sadly run down and the church neglected and ruinous. But as I stood there I remembered some words of Kierkegaard: 'Only the past which can become the present is worth remembering.' Could what happened in the past reverberate and the light once more shine out from this little island? Could the church here again extend itself to encourage others to seek to live holy lives?

The events which led to the founding of Lindisfarne's monastery by Aidan began in 634. Oswald, son of the famously ferocious king Aethelfrith, had taken refuge on Iona following his father's death in the battle for control of Northumbria, and had become a devout Christian. He was determined to march against the pagan Penda of Mercia who had formed an unlikely alliance with the British Christian Cadwallon of Gwynedd. The place where Oswald waited to encounter the enemy was Heavenfield, on Hadrian's Wall near Hexham. It was said that here Oswald had a vision of St Columba telling him to remember the words of God to Joshua as he crossed the Jordan: 'Be strong and courageous; do not be frightened or dismayed, for the Lord your God is with you wherever you go' (Joshua 1.9). Columba told Oswald he would be victorious and reign happily over the land.

Before the battle, Oswald made a cross of two roughly hewn trees and held it while it was placed in the ground. There is no doubt that Oswald wanted to be a Christian king, and perhaps saw himself in the mould of the emperor Constantine, as one who would conquer in the power of Christ. But in the eyes of Cadwallon and his men, Oswald was one of the pagan English, threatening the very way of life of this country. Oswald advanced on the enemy under cover of darkness and caught his foes unprepared. Cadwallon was killed and others fled in panic. Penda survived and would be a constant threat.

This victory brought a new era to Northumbria, for Oswald was convinced that the kingdom would benefit from the Christian faith and education. Perhaps he realized that Christianity could be a truly uniting and healing factor between the English and the Britons. He sent to Iona for teachers in the faith, and the abbot, Segene, immediately dispatched a contingent of monks under the leadership of Corman to Bamburgh castle. But things did not go well. Perhaps Corman's mistake was to set up in a garrison and have hardened soldiers around him – living in barracks is not terribly conducive to a prayer life. Whatever the case, Corman was soon to return to Iona much dispirited, saying that he had been unsuccessful because the English were 'an ungovernable people and of an obstinate and barbarous temperament'. Such words about these early Northumbrians have never endeared Corman to me.

Abbot Segene was obviously disappointed. Realizing how much Oswald wanted his kingdom to be a Christian one, and seeing this as an opportunity the Church should not miss, he called a conference. In the course of discussion, Aidan, an Irishman, stood up and addressed Corman:

> 'Brother, it seems to me that you were too hard on your ignorant hearers. You should have followed the practice of the Apostles, and begun by giving them the milk of simpler teaching, and gradually nourished them with the word of God until they were capable of greater perfection and able to follow the loftier precepts of Christ.' (Bede, *A History*, p. 149)

I imagine Corman would have felt quite stung at this. If he did not say it, he must have been thinking, 'All right, clever one, if you think you can do better, why not go and see how you get on?'

Bede continues:

> At this the faces and the eyes of all who were at the conference were turned towards [Aidan]; and they paid close attention to all that he said, and realized that here was a fit person to be made a bishop and sent to instruct the ignorant and unbeliev-ing, since he was particularly endowed with the grace of dis-cretion, the mother of all virtues. They therefore consecrated him bishop, and sent him to preach. Time would show that Aidan was remarkable not only for discretion but for other virtues as well. (Bede, *A History*, p. 149)

Bede describes Corman as 'austere' and in comparison says of Aidan, 'he was a man of outstanding gentleness, holiness, and moderation. He had a zeal in God' (Bede, *A History*, p. 144). Corman was obviously a powerful man, well able to stand firm in his belief, and tough towards those who differed with him. But austerity is rarely attractive. Too often Christianity is pre-sented as something solemn and diminishing when it needs to be appealing and enhancing, and it is vital we communicate that Jesus came so we might have abundant life. In the delight-ful words of G. K. Chesterton, 'Angels can fly because they take themselves lightly'! It is not the individual who tries to compel us to believe, but the one who attracts us to the faith who makes the lasting impression. One of the great privileges I had on Holy Island was the opportunity to share with many pilgrims and seekers the joy of knowing God and his love.

Aidan decided early on that he would not stay in the garri-son at Bamburgh: not only was it an unfit place for monks who wanted to maintain the round of daily worship, but it aligned them too closely with the ruling power and therefore could cause offence to the indigenous British. Many of these were either lapsed Christians or in need of instruction; others were unbelievers, though it would appear that a large number had a hunger for God.

It was customary for a bishop to have a horse and to ride around the area he served, but this put you above people, and Aidan wanted to meet others at their own level, so he chose to walk. He sought not to possess things or people but to share with all. Whenever he was given money he offered it to others or used it to buy slaves and then set them free. Some of the slaves chose to stay at Lindisfarne and become part of the monastery; some even trained to become priests, there being no discrimination against ex-slaves taking instruction with nobles and sharing with royalty. Rather, everyone was accepted and welcomed.

Lindisfarne was close enough to the centre of power at Bamburgh for Aidan to keep in constant contact and to influence policy. Being on 'the main road' (i.e. the sea), the monks could reach out all over the kingdom. But while committed to working towards Oswald's vision, they also had to grapple with a number of practicalities: houses and a church needed to be built, and farming and fishing organized in a way that would allow the community to be self-sufficient. It was a tall order and called for a sorting of priorities. Aidan and his monks spent much time in prayer, to witness that it was God to whom they sought to consecrate the land; it was he who would send them to share with others that special otherworldly feeling that living on Lindisfarne evoked.

When Aidan went out from Lindisfarne, he carried in his heart the book of Psalms and the gospel, which he had learnt as an act of worship. It was his devotion to the Word of God that served as the basis of his teaching: people saw that he was not telling them to do something he did not practise, but rather inviting them to share in his own experience of the love of God. The message was 'Do as I do: come and enjoy the delights that I enjoy.'

On the island I would often have the pleasure of teaching groups to meditate, to rejoice in the presence, and rest in the peace, of God. Every day we would have at least three acts of worship – sometimes as many as seven or eight – when we would recite psalms and spend time in silent adoration. I was grateful for the years I had been in training with a religious community. The rhythm of prayer gives a balance to life just as the rhythm of the tides on Lindisfarne gives a balance to the island. Personally, I believe in the wisdom of the advice from the Rule of Columba, 'Live near a city but not in it'. Action and involvement are necessary but should be based on prayer and stillness. You cannot proclaim the gospel if you do not spend time getting to know the risen Christ, and too often the Church has sent people out to proclaim the gospel who are well versed in scripture but do not have a deep personal relationship with their God. As Gandhi commented, 'Oh, I do not reject your Christ. I love your Christ. It is just that so many of you Christians are unlike your Christ.'

By 1997, my seventh year on the island, I had spoken to over fifty thousand children and seen more than a million people through the church doors. The opportunities for outreach and sharing in worship were endless. Many school groups, church visits and pilgrimages had been booked for the months ahead, and on one day the island would be invaded by at least sixty bus loads of people, from the Church Army, the Third Order of St Francis, and the parish of Guisborough! I had the challenge of ensuring each group would find a place of peace and quiet amid the crowds, though I had no doubt the island would work its usual wonders.

One evening that year, the fourteenth centenary of the death of St Columba and the beginning of the mission of St Augustine to Britain, I made my way towards the church. The Northern Cross pilgrims from Carlisle, Hexham and Haddington, who had walked over moor and byroad carrying life-sized crosses, were joining other pilgrims to celebrate Easter. No lights would be put on this Holy Saturday evening:

the gathering gloom was a symbol of life without Christ, reminding us that we could suddenly be plunged into darkness without or within. We heard scriptures of promise, sang hymns we knew without books, and, after what seemed an age, went out into the night. As we began to descend a rocky road, I was thankful for the small illumination afforded by the moon and the clearly visible Hale-Bopp comet (which we would not see again for 2,380 years). All these things were good symbols of the spiritual journey: we are often in the dark, feeling that life is a bit rough and that we are going downhill.

But then we turned a corner to face the sea, and there on the shore facing Cuthbert's Island blazed the flames of the Easter fire. The events on the shore of Galilee meant that on the shore of Lindisfarne, on the shore of the world, on the shore of our lives, and on the shore of eternity, the Light of Christ was breaking through to dispel the darkness of the night. I approached the fire with due respect and caution, knowing I could be burned. In a white alb, wearing the white stole with Aidan and Cuthbert worked upon it, I had to light a large Easter Candle from the blaze. Both wax and I melted a little, but I managed on the third attempt. Then those wonderful words: 'May the Christ risen in glory scatter the darkness from our hearts and minds and from this world. Alleluia! Christ is risen, Alleluia! He is risen indeed, Alleluia!' After a few short prayers, we turned back towards the church, and at the entrance to the building everyone lit a candle from the Easter Candle. Light now filled the church, as we prayed that the 'Light of Christ' would fill our lives.

I thought of and gave thanks for all who have passed on the light: Columba, Augustine and especially Aidan, whose statue – with burning torch in hand – stands within the churchyard. Bishop Lightfoot of Durham, when wishing to express the contribution of St Aidan, not only to the Northern part of England, but to the wider reaches of this land through those who went out in mission from Lindisfarne, penned a very memorable phrase: 'Augustine was the Apostle of Kent, but Aidan was the Apostle of England.'

Bishop Lightfoot was not the first to link the two, for Bede gives us a comparison through his *History of the English Church and People*. First he tells of Augustine's dealings with the British bishops, who wondered whether they should abandon their own traditions as Augustine demanded. They were advised by a wise hermit: 'If Augustine is meek and lowly in heart, it shows that he bears the yoke of Christ himself, and offers it to you. But if he is haughty and unbending, then he is not of God and we should not listen to him.' When the bishops enquired how they would know which was the case, the hermit advised them to let Augustine and his contingent arrive first, 'then if he rises to meet you when you approach rest assured that he is a servant of Christ, but if he ignores you and does not rise, since you are in the majority, do not comply with his demands'. As it happened, Augustine did not rise to greet the British bishops but remained seated, determined to show his power and authority. As ever, when force meets force there is nothing but trouble ahead. It might seem a trivial matter but it was his dealing with the bishops, who were part of the country before he arrived, that slowed down the progress with the indigenous British wing of the church. What a contrast to Aidan, who sought unity and peace with all.

The early foundation on Lindisfarne must have been very simple. Surrounding the site would be a low wall, too low to keep out armies or even wild animals, but symbolic as a barrier against evil. All within was holy, not only the little wooden church and the dwellings and the work places, but each person and each task. Everything was dedicated to God for everything belonged to God. It is likely that each monk had his own simply built wooden cell and he would share this with a student under his guidance and teaching. Unlike the Roman style of tonsure, these monks shaved the front of their heads from ear to ear and let their hair grow long at the back, in the style of

Celtic warriors. This was to witness that they were 'soldiers for Christ' and dedicated in his service. It was a hard life and called for well-honed young men, not afraid to face considerable danger in fulfilling their mission.

In the early years, Aidan obviously had difficulty with the language of the English. Bede tells us that there were originally twelve English students on Lindisfarne, and we know the names of five of them: Eata, who would become abbot of Melrose and then abbot of Lindisfarne, and the four brothers Chad, Cedd, Caelin and Cynibil. However, it would have been much easier for Aidan to communicate with the British who shared a similar Celtic dialect. When he preached the gospel to the English, none other than King Oswald acted as his interpreter, in order that his thanes and leaders could hear the good news too. With a king so ready to help it is not surprising that Aidan's mission flourished, though his own character played a large part: people saw that he practised what he preached and had an enthusiasm that could only be of God. Bede tells how many Scots (as the Irish were then known) arrived day by day to proclaim the word of God in the provinces under Oswald's rule. People were baptized, and Oswald gave generously for the building of churches and monasteries from his own riches. The light of Christ was spreading out from Lindisfarne: monasteries were built at Melrose, St Abb's Head and at Hexham. In 646 another was created at Hartlepool by Heiu, the first woman in Northumbria to become a nun. Aidan persuaded Hilda, a relative of King Edwin of Northumbria (with whom she had been baptized in York by Bishop Paulinus), to remain in the kingdom rather than join her sister at the monastery of Chelles in France. Hilda was given a hide of land (between 60 and 120 acres) on the north side of the River Wear where she kept the monastic life. Then Hilda went to be in charge of the monastery at Hartlepool as Heiu moved to found yet another monastery at Kaelcacaestir, which is possibly present-day Tadcaster. After some years Hilda herself moved on and established another monastery at Streanaeshalch, later known as Whitby.

Aidan would often come to Bamburgh, to celebrate communion and to talk over policy with Oswald. During this time he was aware of the king's deep piety: Oswald rose early in the morning to say his prayers, often before the break of day, when he would sit with his hands open facing upwards and resting on his knees. Aidan was well aware how generous these hands were.

One Easter Aidan had gone to the castle to celebrate the festival. Normally on these occasions, he ate frugally and escaped from the noise of the feasting hall as soon as possible to pray in quiet with his brethren. But this Easter, just as the best food was being served up on a silver dish and a blessing asked upon it, a nervous-looking servant suddenly appeared in the doorway. He told the king that there was a great company of poor people gathering outside. The winter had been hard and the meagre resources they lived on had run out: they were starving. Oswald stood up, and pointing to the silver dish laden with food said, 'Take this out to them, see that they all get some food.' He paused slightly and then continued, 'And give to them the silver dish that the food is on. See that it is divided up among them so that they have something for another day.' The servant who was delegated to look after the poor did not know what to say. He bowed before Oswald and then walked out, two servants following with the great silver dish. Aidan was deeply moved by such generosity, and, taking hold of the open hand of Oswald, said, 'May this hand never wither with age.'

Not long afterwards, aged only 38, Oswald was killed in the battle of Maserfeld by his old enemy Penda.

In Bernicia, the northern part of Northumbria, Oswy, Oswald's brother, was immediately proclaimed king – there had never been any doubt that Oswy would rule the northern kingdom. In the south, Oswy's cousin Oswin took control of Deira, and the great kingdom of Northumbria was divided once more. However, both these rulers were favourable towards Lindisfarne and the Christian mission. Oswy, of course, had been on Iona with Oswald: he was a spirited leader who saw the benefits of having Aidan and his monks so near to him, and wanted Lindisfarne to continue to flourish. He hoped for more schools and teaching for his leaders on their various estates. Aidan was free to go wherever he pleased and to continue his good works, and this could only be for the benefit of the kingdom.

Within a year of beginning to rule Bernicia, Oswy marched with an army and retrieved the body of Oswald, which had been quartered and put on spikes. His head was taken to Lindisfarne to be buried and his hands and arms brought back to Bamburgh. In fulfilment of Aidan's prophecy, these remained uncorrupt, as relics to be venerated. In time Oswald became an important saint in a good part of Europe.

Aidan was greatly surprised when Oswy told him he was going marry the princess, Eanfled, the daughter of Edwin. Oswy already had a love child, Aldfrith, whose mother, the Irish princess Fina, was the sister of Finan with whom Aidan had worked at Iona. It was already rumoured that one day Aldfrith could be king, and Aidan was pleased at this thought, for Aldfrith was getting his schooling in the monasteries of Ireland. Oswy had later married the great-granddaughter of Urien, Rhianmelt, who was known as 'Queen of Lightning', and so united the kingdom of Rheged with that of Bernicia. Of this marriage was born Alchfrith. As Rhianmelt was now dead, Oswy was free to take Eanfled as his wife. In doing so, Oswy was aiming at a political alliance as much as a marriage: in marrying Edwin's daughter he had a rightful claim to Deira, as Edwin had been king of the whole of Northumbria. This did not bode well for Oswin in the south.

———◆———

In order to maintain balance in his life during these turbulent times, Aidan would often retreat to the nearest of the Farne islands off Bamburgh for prayer and stillness. It was said that the island was inhabited by demons, small dark creatures that put fear into any who ventured there, but Aidan regarded this as a challenge. As a witness to the power of God, through prayer, he would ward off the demons and banish them.

Around 650, Aidan was on the island when he saw a great deal of activity going on at Bamburgh. An army was marching towards the city, and it was obvious they were invaders – no doubt the old enemy Penda and his Mercian forces on the warpath. Aidan hoped that the people of the village had fled into the castle for safety, for Penda would show no mercy. Bamburgh castle was so well defended by its rocky approach that Aidan was almost sure Oswy and Eanfled would be safe.

Penda's men started tearing the village to pieces, hauling the thatch off the cottages, pulling out beams, rafters and wattle walls, and carrying them up to the palace gates. Here a great heap of combustible material was gathered for the purposes of burning down the gate and wooden palisade, and so breaking into the palace. The wind was in Penda's favour and he ordered the fire to be lit. Smoke was blowing into the palace and high into the air. Inside eyes were streaming, and many were already suffering from inhaling so much smoke. There were signs of excitement and joy from Penda and his warriors. Soon another king of Northumbria would be no more, and Penda would be inside the great fortress of Oswy.

Two miles away, Aidan saw the smoke rising and guessed at the trouble. In a loud voice he prayed the only prayer we have on record, saying simply, 'Lord, see what evil Penda does.' As he spoke, Aidan felt a change in the air around him. The wind suddenly started gusting from the north-east. With joy he watched the smoke being blown away from the palace and across the land. Penda's troops, on the other hand, were no longer joyful! Their eyes and lungs were filled: it was as if the very elements had turned against them. They had no option but to retreat.

Oswin ruled the southern half of Northumbria, Deira, for seven years. He was, according to Bede, of

> handsome appearance, lofty in stature, pleasant in speech and courteous in manner. He was generous to high and low alike, and soon won the affection of everyone ... So that nobles came from almost every province to enter his service. But among his other special endowments of virtue and moderation the greatest was what one might describe as the singular blessing of humility. (Bede, *A History*, p. 164)

At this stage in history these were not particularly admirable qualities in an English king, as people desired warrior kings to battle against warring neighbours. However, English kings were expected to be generous, and Oswin was appreciated for his giving to rich and poor alike. In fact, he won the affection of many by his kindness and his regal qualities of mind and body. Nobles came to serve him from all over the province, his humility being a characteristic so often missing in the royal court. Though far from Lindisfarne, we know that Aidan visited Oswin on more than one occasion in his efforts to spread the gospel and to keep peace in the land.

For all that Aidan sought peace, it was not long before Oswy acted on his belief that Bernicia and Deira needed to be united in order to do battle against the old enemy Penda, and that he, Oswy, should rule the whole of Northumbria. He mustered his army and marched south to Wilfar's Dun near Catterick. Oswin, realizing that the stronger Bernician army would triumph over Deira's troops, disbanded them, as there seemed no sense in allowing his people to be killed unnecessarily. Oswin then went into hiding along with a nobleman called Tondhere and a close and trusted friend named Hunwald. But Hunwald betrayed Oswin by letting Oswy know where the fugitives could be found. Oswy's representative, Aethelwin, was sent then to assassinate both Tondhere and Oswin, and they died in a place called Gilling on 20 August 651. A Christian king had caused the murder of another. This shameful deed alienated the two

31

kingdoms still further and did nothing to help Oswy, as ruler of both, in his desire for more power.

Aidan was deeply distressed, as was Oswy's wife Eanfled, who swore her husband would need to make reparation for the murder of this kind and gracious ruler. As Aidan approached Bamburgh to speak to Oswy, his mind went back over the last sixteen years. How much had happened, what wonderful things God had brought to pass! Throughout the kingdom there were centres of worship and places of learning. All down the coast, at every river mouth, there was a Christian settlement and often a monastery. Churches and wayside crosses had sprung up all over the place. Education and art were growing as were the numbers of the faithful. God had greatly blessed this land and had used Bamburgh and Lindisfarne to achieve much. Now all was in danger. The thought caused a great pain to shoot through Aidan's chest. The encounter he would have with Oswy troubled him though it was necessary for the good of Northumbria and for the soul of the king.

The fortress loomed ahead of him on the great outcrop of rock. The light was beginning to fade. But another darkness was also coming upon Aidan. He could hardly breathe and his heart ached. As he came to Bamburgh church it was noticed that Aidan was ill and a little tent was erected for him outside the west end of the building. Lying there looking across to his beloved Lindisfarne, on 31 August 651, only eleven days after the murder of Oswin, Aidan passed away.

His body was taken across to Lindisfarne and buried in the monks' cemetery. When a larger church was built on the island, Aidan's bones were transferred to it and buried at the right side of the altar in accordance with the honours due to so holy and revered a bishop. Though a great light had gone out that August day, the light of the Good News was still spreading throughout the land. Way out on the hills to the north, a young 16-year-old had a vision that would do much to fan the flames.

The Keys of the Kingdom

'And I tell you, you are Peter, and on this rock I will build my church, and the gates of Hades will not prevail against it. I will give to you the keys of the kingdom of heaven, and whatever you bind on earth will be bound in heaven, and whatever you loose on earth will be loosed in heaven.'

(Matthew 16.18–19)

I have a large ancient key, acquired many years ago, which is more than ten inches long and was hand-forged by a blacksmith out of a single piece of metal. One end of the key is shaped like a clover leaf, in a Celtic pattern, to symbolize the Trinity. Quite wonderfully, after having this key for about twenty years, I found when I moved to Lindisfarne that it opened and locked the church door. Keys are often a symbol of authority and power, for they give the holder some control over a building or a treasure. As I held this ancient key, which had waited so long to be used, I felt encouraged to trust in my ability to care for this sacred place.

Prior to moving to Lindisfarne, I lived on the North Yorkshire Moors and looked after an ancient church dedicated to St Hilda. St Hilda was inspired by the teachings of Aidan, and in 1980 we celebrated the thirteenth centenary of her death with a service in Whitby Abbey. I was at Whitby too for the first meeting of the York diocesan synod, and couldn't resist asking to have the minutes of the previous synod read. The secretary rose to the bait and said there were none, but in fact there is quite a good set of minutes in Bede's *History of the English Church and People* dating from 664!

Between the death of Aidan in 651 and the coming of Cuthbert to Lindisfarne in 664, much would happen to the island community and the church at large. Finan succeeded Aidan as bishop on Lindisfarne and continued the work of outreach. One of the amazing events of his episcopate was the baptism of Peada, the son of the old pagan warrior Penda of Mercia. Penda had appointed his son to the kingship of the Middle Angles, and Peada sought to marry Alchfled, a daughter of Oswy. No doubt with some influence from Bishop Finan, Oswy would only agree to the marriage if Peada and his people accepted the Christian faith. Surprisingly, Peada, once instructed, said he would gladly become a Christian, even if he were refused by the princess. Peada, his companions, thanes and all their servants were baptized by Finan at a village owned by Oswy and known as At-Wall, which was by Hadrian's Wall. When Peada returned to his kingdom he took with him four priests from Lindisfarne, Cedd, Adda, Betti and Diuma. The light that Aidan had lit, the Light of Christ, was spreading further afield.

A little later Sigbert, king of the East Saxons, accepted the faith through the influence of Oswy who was his friend. Sigbert was also baptized by Bishop Finan at the royal villa at At-Wall. Here Bede tells us how Oswy, who had a firm grasp of the faith from his schooling on Iona and then at Bamburgh (despite ordering the murder of Oswin!), witnessed to Sigbert, saying something like this:

> God is boundless in his majesty, though invisible to the
> human eye.
> God is Almighty, Creator of heaven and earth and of all the
> human race.
> In justice he rules and will judge the world.
> He abides in eternity, not in perishable metals and idols.
> All who know and do the will of their Creator will receive
> eternal life.

Oswy saw in the growth of Christianity a hope for unity and peace throughout the land, and asked Cedd to come from the kingdom of Mercia in the Midlands, and go with another priest to evangelize the East Saxons. On reporting back to Lindisfarne, Cedd was consecrated bishop for the East Saxons.

He then returned to Essex and continued to build churches and two monasteries and to ordain priests and deacons. While on a visit to Northumbria he built a third monastery at Lastingham in North Yorkshire. The Church was growing but within it there was unrest, for as the monasteries stretched out from Lindisfarne as far as Essex and close to London, they came in conflict with those believers whose allegiance was to Rome. Two parts of the one Church were expressing their faith in different ways, and it was obvious that some of their differences needed to be reconciled for the sake of unity and outreach in the land.

One difficulty was the method used to calculate the date of Easter. The old Celtic way had been superseded on the continent by a more modern method. This meant that in Oswy's royal household at Bamburgh, Queen Eanfled, who followed the Roman calendar, celebrated Easter at a different time from her husband. Oswy would be feasting while Eanfled was still fasting! Things would come to a head in 665, when the dates of Easter were as far apart as they could be. Other points of contention were that the Celtic monks had a different type of tonsure from the Roman ones, and that their practices of baptism differed, as did their consecration of bishops and the place of bishops within the monastic household. Obviously matters needed to be resolved for the sake of the whole Church.

The question, as much as any, was who should be in charge. There was no doubt that once linked with Rome, the indigenous branch would lose overall control of the Church in Britain: often major decisions would be made by 'foreigners' who had never been to its shores. (Some parallels may be drawn with Britain's membership of the European Union.) Large is not always better, and loss of independence and age-old traditions would be hard.

In Northumbria one of the champions of Rome was an Irishman named Ronan, who had been to Gaul and Italy for part of his education. Bede tells us Ronan convinced many to look more closely at the Roman way of calculating Easter, 'but he entirely failed to persuade Finan the bishop of Lindisfarne, a hot-tempered man whom reproof made more obstinate and openly hostile to the truth'. But then you know which side Bede was on!

James the deacon, who had come north with Paulinus, the bishop of York, was still in Deira and keeping the Roman Easter. Queen Eanfled was ministered to by her own priest, Romanus, who followed Canterbury and Rome. Oswy's son, Alchfrith, removed from Ripon both Eata, abbot of Melrose who had been appointed to form a monastery there, and Cuthbert (of whom more shortly), who had accompanied him, because they were not prepared to adopt 'catholic' ways. He then gave the monastery, with forty hides of land, to his great friend Wilfrid and appointed him abbot. Wilfrid was an English monk who had received some early training on Lindisfarne, but was much influenced by his time in Rome and Lyon. Alchfrith clearly thought the authority of the Roman branch of the Church was greater than that of the Celtic, Iona, branch.

War with Penda was still an issue even though Peada had become a Christian. Oswy remembered well that Penda had killed his brother Oswald, and at first tried to buy peace with Penda on the condition that he stopped ravaging the land. This failed and Oswy knew he had to stop the old enemy once and for all. Before their final battle Oswy promised that if he was victorious, he would dedicate his daughter Elfled to God by giving her to a monastery. He would also endow the church of Lindisfarne with twelve estates each of ten hides. All this was in penance for the killing of Oswin at Gilling, and, in addition, Queen Eanfled persuaded her husband to give land at Gilling itself for the building of a monastery. Another of the newly formed monasteries of ten hides was likely to have been the double one, for men and women, at the 'bay of the lighthouse', that is, at Whitby. Here Abbess Hilda would receive the infant daughter of Oswy.

The Church's ownership of land was increasing like never before; the gospel was spreading throughout the country, and

Wilfrid and the Roman wing of the Church were growing in power. Agilbert, bishop of the West Saxons, who was from Gaul, was friendly with Wilfrid and with Oswy's son, Alchfrith. He came to Northumbria for a while and brought with him a learned priest called Agatho. Between them they persuaded Oswy to call a church synod so that decisions about church unity and government could be ironed out.

This meeting was well recorded as it was of such importance. The year was 664 and the place Whitby Abbey. On the Celtic side, the leading participants were Colman, now bishop of Lindisfarne following Finan's death in 661 (and helpfully somewhat less aggressive than his predecessor), Hilda and Cedd, who acted as interpreter for both parties. Representing Rome and Canterbury were Bishop Agilbert, the priests Agatho, Wilfrid and Romanus, and James the deacon, now an elderly man.

King Oswy opened the proceedings by observing that all who serve the one God should observe one rule of life and that they should not differ in the celebrating of the sacraments. The one Church should show its unity. Oswy then directed his own bishop, Colman, to speak first. Colman said:

> The Easter customs which I observe were taught me by my superiors, who sent me here as bishop: and all our forefathers, men beloved of God, are known to have observed these customs. And lest anyone condemn or reject them as wrong, it is recorded that they owe their origin to the blessed evangelist Saint John, the disciple especially loved by our Lord, and all the churches over which he presided. (Bede, *A History*, p. 188)

Agilbert was then invited to speak on behalf of the Roman party but he declined with the excuse that he wanted Wilfrid, who was fluent in English and would not need an interpreter, to speak in his place. As Wilfrid was a friend of Alchfrith and Eanfled this was a clever move: he was also a very gifted and forceful speaker. Wilfrid said how their Easter customs were those observed by Rome, where Peter and Paul lived and taught. The same customs were held throughout Gaul and Italy, as well as Africa, Asia, Egypt, Greece and throughout the world. He then said how the Celtic Christians stood alone – 'The only people stupid enough to disagree with the whole world.'

Colman rose and defended his people against this jibe of stupidity, falling back on the teaching of John and also that of Columba. Wilfrid replied with the smoothness of a politician. He gave Columba and the Celtic saints the slightest of praise but pointed out that they were still in error:

> For, although your Fathers were holy men, do you imagine that they, a few men in a corner of a remote island, are to be pre-ferred before the universal Church of Christ throughout the world? And even if your Columba – or, may I say, ours also if he was the servant of Christ – was a saint potent in miracles, can he take precedence before the most blessed Prince of the Apostles, to who our Lord said: 'Thou art Peter, and upon this rock I will build my Church, and the gates of hell shall not pre-vail against it, and I will give unto thee the keys of the kingdom of heaven'? (Bede, *A History*, p. 192)

With mention of the 'keys of the kingdom' Wilfrid had scored match point (though some wondered among themselves quite which kingdom he was after). Perhaps from the outset Oswy was hoping for a result that would bring peace in his household as well as within the Church. Turning to Colman and Wilfrid, he asked if they agreed that Peter held the keys to the kingdom of heaven. Colman could only acknowledge these were the words of our Lord to Peter. They both answered, 'We do.' Then Oswy concluded the meeting saying:

> Then, I tell you, Peter is guardian of the gates of heaven, and I shall not contradict him, I shall obey his commands in every-thing to the best of my knowledge and ability; otherwise, when I come to the gates of heaven, there may be no one to open them, because he who holds the keys has turned away.
> (Bede, *A History*, p. 192)

Within the meeting Oswy got all to agree that they would accept Roman ways and discipline and that the Church in Northumbria would display a united front. But according to Wilfrid's biographer, Eddius Stephanus, Bishop Colman was told that if, out of respect for his own country's customs, he should reject the Roman tonsure and method of calculating Easter, he was to resign his see in favour of another and better candidate! After the meeting Colman did indeed decide he could no longer stay within the church of Northumbria. Only thirty years after Aidan's arrival on Lindisfarne, there was to be a massive power shift towards Canterbury and Rome, and no doubt Colman felt that in losing the debate he had let the mission from Iona down. He resigned, and asked King Oswy if he might appoint Eata, one of Aidan's own men, as bishop of Lindisfarne. But instead Tuda, who was trained in southern Ireland, had a Roman tonsure and kept the Roman Easter, was appointed. Colman duly left for Iona, accompanied by many loyal monks and carrying some of the bones of St Aidan. However, the plague that was rife in 664 killed Tuda after only a few months, and Eata was then appointed to Lindisfarne in his place. Eata decided to have the prior of Melrose join him and so it was that Cuthbert came to the island.

As a reward for his expertise at the Synod of Whitby, Wilfrid was to be made a bishop, with a see centred on York. The bishop of Lindisfarne would never again have oversight of the whole of Northumbria.

Wilfrid asked if he might go to Gaul to be consecrated as he did not want the formal proceedings to involve any bishops who might be of the Celtic persuasion. It could be he was really looking for more ritual, pomp and ceremony than he would have got in Britain. He was consecrated at Compiegne in Gaul, and at least fourteen bishops, including his friend and mentor Agilbert, were present. Wilfrid was carried on a golden throne and protected by an army of 120 soldiers. This display of power and riches was much in contrast to the simplicity of Lindisfarne, which Wilfrid knew well. Indeed, when Colman departed for Iona, Bede wrote:

> So frugal and austere were Colman and his predecessors that when they left the seat of their authority there were very few buildings except the church; indeed no more than met the bare requirements of a seemly way of life. They had no property except cattle and whenever they received any money from rich folk, they immediately gave it away to the poor; for they had no need to amass money or provide lodging for important people, since such visited the church only in order to pray or hear the word of God. Whenever the opportunity offered, the king himself used to come with only five or six attendants; and when he had completed his prayers in the church, he used to leave. But if they happened to remain for a meal, they were content with the plain daily food of brothers and asked nothing more. In those days the sole concern of these teachers was to serve God, not the world; to satisfy the soul not the belly. Accordingly the religious habit at that time was held in high esteem. Whenever any priest or monk paid a visit, he was joyfully welcomed by all as a servant of God. And if people met him on the road, they ran to him and bowed eager to be signed by his hand or receive a blessing from his lips. Whenever he spoke the word of encouragement, he was given an attentive hearing. On Sundays the people flocked to the churches and monasteries, not to obtain food but to hear the word of God. When a priest visited a village, the people were quick to gather together to receive the word of life; for the priests and clerics always came to a village solely to preach, baptize, visit the sick, and, in short, to care for the souls of its people. They were so free from the sin of avarice that none of them would accept lands or gifts for the building of monasteries unless expressly directed to do so by the secular authorities. (Bede, *A History*, pp. 194–5)

Though in many ways Lindisfarne had been downgraded, it would prosper like never before. The synthesis of Celtic, Anglo-Saxon and Roman artistic traditions would enrich the Church. Above all else it would be the influence of Cuthbert, in life and death, that would lead Lindisfarne to be described as 'the holiest place in holy England'. Yet its new enrichment would also make it an attractive and easy target for raiders from overseas. If the Vikings had attacked Aidan's island, they would have found little to take away.

The plague of 664 caused the deaths of both the Archbishop of Canterbury and his appointed successor in Rome. Theodore of Tarsus, a monk from the birthplace of St Paul, was chosen by the pope as the new archbishop. As he came from the east, he did not have a Roman tonsure and waited four months in Rome so that his hair could grow sufficiently to receive one! Although he was 66 years old, Theodore had great vitality and organizing power and would be archbishop for 21 years. He travelled throughout England, organizing it into dioceses and, where necessary, splitting the larger dioceses into smaller ones. The diocesan system that the Church of England holds today is very much due to his foundation.

There is no doubt that Theodore made sure people knew who was in control and that the Church in England conformed to the practices of Rome. Soon after succeeding Aidan, Finan had built a new church on Lindisfarne, 'suitable for an episcopal see', in the Celtic style of hewn oak with a thatched roof. Theodore rededicated it to St Peter. He told Chad that he had not received a 'regular' consecration as bishop and removed him from York, though on accepting a 're-consecration', Chad was soon made bishop of Mercia. Perhaps it was also about this time that the stone was placed at Whithorn, which simply declares 'The place of the Apostle Peter'.

————◆◆◆————

It was just before 5.00 a.m. on a summer's morning but I was up and ready to use the great 'Celtic' clover-shaped key to open the outer door to St Mary's. I did this early every day in summer for the sake of the swallows that nested in the porch. I would not lock the church until after 11.00 p.m., so the swallows would have plenty of time to feed their young. This early start allowed me to enjoy the quietness within: the building was already blazing brightly in the shining sun, and I knelt there in its radiance.

Cuthbert Afire with Love

But fain St Hilda's nuns would learn
If on a rock by Lindisfarne
St Cuthbert sits and toils to frame
The sea-borne beads that bear his name.
Such tales had Whitby's fishers told,
And said they might his shape behold,
And hear his anvil sound:
A deadening clang, – a huge dim form
Seen but and heard when gathering storm
And night were closing round.
              (Walter Scott, *Marmion*, p. 44)

I took a small group of children to look for Cuthbert's beads. Legend says they were made by Cuthbert and sometimes strung together to make a rosary. As millions have been collected, they are now not so easy to come across, but we managed to find enough good specimens for each child to have one. Most about the size of a pea, the beads are the fossilized remains of a species of crinoid, or feather-star, that was around in the palaeozoic era – a bit before Cuthbert's time! But the adventure of seeking and finding them is always a joy.

We then walked onto the little island just off Lindisfarne, which has the ancient name of Hobthrush but is better known as Cuthbert's Island. Suddenly we heard the sound, 'Oo, ah-oo, hoo, Oo, ah-oo, hoo'. It sounded like a company of respectable ladies responding to a naughty story! But I knew it would be a small group of eider drakes talking to each other, and moved over to see them: such beautiful birds in their black and white plumage with green on the nape and side of the neck. The few ducks with the drakes, by contrast, were a mottled brown. The eider ducks are locally known as 'Cuddy ducks' because they were once looked after and protected by St Cuthbert. It was to this tiny island he would come to be alone. He had a very small cell, the remains of which may be the heap of stones on the island, and there is also a small ruined medieval chapel which I explored with the children. We admired the campion, thrift and wild thyme growing out of its low walls.

Cuthbert was just what the English Church in the north needed – a local home-grown saint who embodied something of their heroic temperament. Aidan could not fit the bill because he was Celtic! But Cuthbert personified the Celtic and the Roman branches of the Church, united and enriched by each other. Here is Bede, who wrote a wonderful life of the saint, on Cuthbert at eight years old:

> He was agile by nature and quick witted, he very often used to prevail over his rivals in play, so that sometimes, when the rest were tired, he, being still untired, would triumphantly look around to see whether any were willing to contend with him again. Whether they were jumping or running or wrestling or exercising their limbs in any other way, he used to boast that he had beaten all who were his equals and even some who were older.

> (Bertram Colgrave, *Two Lives of Cuthbert*, Cambridge University Press, 1985, p. 157)

It was on one such sporting occasion that a child of three spoke to Cuthbert as if he were an old man: 'Why O Cuthbert, most holy bishop and priest, do you do these things so contrary to your nature and rank?' A prophecy? At least it tells us that in the year 643, Cuthbert lived in a Christian community and even the children knew of priests and bishops. Bede saw this occasion for Cuthbert as the time when 'the ears of his heart had been opened' to God. Possibly this had something to do with the foster mother Cuthbert had just acquired, Kenswith, who seems to have been a Christian. Later in life, when widowed, she became a nun.

Being a Christian does not mean you escape the trials of life. The young, strong Cuthbert was soon hardly able to walk due to trouble with his knee, and had to be carried outside to rest in the open air. Here he encountered a horseman – a stranger dressed in white – who examined his injury, recommended a poultice, and then departed as mysteriously as he had arrived. The poultice was made and Cuthbert was healed. He never forgot his 'angel on horseback', and from this time on seems to have been regularly granted angelic assistance in the midst of difficulties.

It was when St Aidan died on 31 August 651 that Cuthbert had a vision and received his call. Then sixteen, he owned a horse and a spear – indicating he was relatively affluent – and had possibly gone into battle for his king. This particular day he was in the Lammermuir hills, minding (in suitably biblical fashion) a flock of sheep by night. Bede writes:

> On a certain night while his companions were sleeping, he himself was keeping watch and praying according to his custom, when he suddenly saw a stream of light from the sky breaking in upon the darkness of the long night. In the midst of this, the choir of the heavenly hosts descending to the earth, and taking with them, without delay, a soul of exceeding brightness, returned to their heavenly home.
>
> (Colgrave, *Two Lives of Cuthbert*, pp. 165–6)

Cuthbert discovered the next day that Aidan had died at Bamburgh, about forty miles away. Such a happening is challenging if not life-changing. Cuthbert went to offer himself at the monastery at Melrose (why he did not go straight to Lindisfarne we do not know) and, as he neared, gave his horse and spear to a servant. The prior, Boisil, stood at the gates watching the young man come forward empty-handed, and said, 'Behold the servant of the Lord.' Possibly Boisil had just been reading St John's Gospel and remembered these as the words Jesus said about Nathanael, but one of the monks standing nearby was most surprised by his prior's reaction! Cuthbert was welcomed and brought into the monastery, but told he could not be admitted formally until the abbot, Eata, one of Aidan's first pupils, returned. Meanwhile Cuthbert learnt the routine that was to become his way of life: a rhythm of prayer, study and manual labour. Here he would learn to love God, and of the love of God, before going out to tell of God.

When Eata returned, Boisil explained he believed Cuthbert was a worthy candidate for the monastic life, and Cuthbert duly received the tonsure and joined the brethren. Cuthbert gave praise to God as his head was ceremoniously shaved in the Celtic style. He knew he was taking part in a great adventure, being allowed to share with the heroes of God. He was stricter on himself than the Rule required, and more diligent in prayer and reading, learning all the 150 psalms and the services off by heart. He often spent the night in prayer, and sometimes even a second and third night, sleeping only on the fourth. He threw himself into manual labour with enthusiasm and his physical strength was of much benefit to the monastery. He fasted for long periods but not to excess, in case he was weakened for the work he had to do. In all things Cuthbert seemed to excel.

Boisil passed on to Cuthbert a deep love for St John's Gospel. Cuthbert not only studied the Gospel but learnt great portions of it off by heart in sheer joy. Both Eata and Boisil were sure that Cuthbert would become a leader of others. He was a man with a future.

After a few years, the community was offered land for another monastery at Ripon in Deira (where Wilfrid, as we have already learnt, would eventually be appointed abbot). Eata went to see to its management, taking Cuthbert with him, and in due course Cuthbert became guestmaster there. His duties included caring for all who called on the monks for help, and it was while at Ripon that he met with an angelic visitor in the guise of a poor man seeking food and shelter. Bede writes of Cuthbert and his caring for others:

> Above all else he was afire with heavenly love, unassumingly patient, devoted to unceasing prayer, and kindly to all who came to him for comfort. He regarded the labour of helping the weaker brethren with advice as equivalent to prayer, remembering that He who said 'Thou shalt love the Lord thy God' also said 'love thy neighbour'.　　　　　(Bede, *A History*, p. 263)

Eventually Cuthbert returned to Melrose and here, along with many others, caught the plague. It seemed Cuthbert would die, and the community decided to pray for him throughout the night. When one of the brethren told Cuthbert of this, he insisted on rising the next morning and trying to walk with the aid of his staff – he was so sure that God would answer the community's prayers. Indeed, Cuthbert slowly recovered his strength from this point on, though he was troubled with some inner pain for the rest of his life.

Boisil was convinced that Cuthbert had been saved for a purpose, and said to him:

> See how you have been delivered from this affliction. You will not be stricken by it again nor will you die now. However, my death is near at hand. I want you to learn from me as long as I am able to teach you. Not more than seven days remain in which I shall have sufficient health of body and strength of tongue to teach you.

Sadly, Cuthbert knew Boisil's words were true. He hid his sorrow by asking, 'What is best for us to read so that we can finish it in a week?' Boisil seemed to gather strength as he replied, 'The evangelist John. I have a book of seven gatherings (so many vellum pages of St John folded together) of which we can go through one gathering each day, with the Lord's help, reading it and discussing it between ourselves so far as it is necessary.' This is what they did, and for Cuthbert it was a very precious time. Not only was he privileged to look after his ailing prior and friend, but Boisil also talked to him about his own future.

Among other things, Boisil told Cuthbert that one day he would be made a bishop. It was strange that way back when he was only eight, a child of three had said the same thing. The idea did not thrill Cuthbert at all: he did not want to get involved in the government of church or state, preferring a quieter, more prayerful life.

It was around 660 when Boisil died, and though now only in his mid twenties, Cuthbert became the prior of Melrose. His days were filled with teaching and spiritual direction, but he also delighted in going out on mission. Often he was away for a month at a time, visiting the deep hill country populated by the indigenous British, where few others ventured to travel. Sometimes he went on horseback; sometimes he travelled by boat; more often he simply walked. Many were drawn to his ministry of preaching and care for the poor: some came to make their confessions and seek forgiveness; others accepted the faith and were baptized; others found freedom from lives bound by superstition and idolatry. If a community had a Christian presence, Cuthbert would celebrate the Eucharist using his portable altar. On most journeys he took a companion, often someone whom he was instructing in the ways of outreach and mission – a reminder of how Jesus sent out his disciples 'two by two'.

On one occasion, Bede relates, Cuthbert and a young monk were journeying southwards along the River Teviot, reciting psalms and portions of the scriptures as they went. An outlying farmstead offered them a meal which Cuthbert declined, telling the family they were fasting. However, he preached the gospel to them and offered a blessing. The two then left for the hill country and had gone a good distance when Cuthbert asked the young man, 'Where will we find food here today?' The boy was at a loss to reply, feeling that there was no one around who could feed them. Cuthbert told him to cheer up and have faith. 'The Lord will provide for us today, as he always does.' Cuthbert then pointed to an eagle flying high overhead. 'See that bird flying high above us. It is possible for God to refresh us by the ministrations of the eagle.' The young man was not sure what Cuthbert was suggesting, but as they travelled further along the river, they saw the eagle settle on the bank with a fish in its claws. 'Run and see what food the eagle has brought us from the Lord.' The young man did so and brought back a large fish that the eagle had just taken from the river. 'What have you done, my son? Why have you not given our handmaiden her share? Cut it quickly in half and take her the share which she deserves for ministering to us.' Doing this, the young man now thought, 'How wonderful, we truly have a rich fare.' Cuthbert said, 'There is more food here than we need. Let us now seek out a poor household and we will share the fish with them. We cannot just keep this to ourselves.' Though the young man was probably a little reluctant, he felt there was something deeper at work here and agreed. They went on until they reached such a household and presented the fish to them. The family broiled the fish and they all shared the meal as Cuthbert shared the gospel with them. There is little wonder that the people of the hill country of Northumbria loved him. In telling this story, Bede would be well aware of its symbolic meaning: the eagle was the symbol for St John's Gospel and the fish, in Greek *ichthus*, was a code name for 'Jesus Christ, Son of God, Saviour'.

On another occasion, Cuthbert was invited to worship with the community of men and women at the abbey of Coldingham, where Ebba was abbess. This monastery stood high on the cliffs overlooking the North Sea, from which Lindisfarne could be seen far away in the south. One night, seeking time for quiet prayer, Cuthbert climbed down the cliffs, secretly followed by one of the brothers who was curious to see what he was up to. He saw Cuthbert wade into the sea until the water was up to his neck: there, with arms outstretched, he spent the night giving praise to God and singing to the sound of the waves. At daybreak, he returned to shore and began to pray again, kneeling on the beach. While he was doing this, two otters ran out of the sea and rubbed themselves against his legs and feet as if to dry them. Cuthbert blessed the creatures, before making his way to the monastic church for the singing of the canonical hymns at their appointed hour.

The watching monk was now filled with fear. He had been privileged to see something special but he was sure Cuthbert was aware of his spying. He approached Cuthbert, stretched himself on the ground and asked for forgiveness. 'What is the matter, brother? What have you done? Have you been spying on me in my nightly vigil?' The poor man was too fearful to respond. Cuthbert then said, 'Brother, you are forgiven but on one condition: that you promise to tell no one of this until after my death.' The promise was given and Cuthbert blessed the brother. After Cuthbert died, he told as many people as he could.

On another occasion, Cuthbert had to make a boat trip northwards to the land of the Picts, probably along the east coast of Fife in Scotland. It was just after Christmas and he and his two companions expected to return quickly in favourable weather, but were caught in a storm and driven ashore. The Epiphany was at hand, and Cuthbert spent the night in prayer. Then he said to his companions:

> Why I ask do we remain inactive and slothful and not seek some way of safety in every direction? Lo! The land is grim with snow and the sky with clouds; the heavens rage with adverse winds and the sea with waves. We ourselves are in want and there is no man to refresh us. So let us importune the Lord with prayers, that as he once opened up a path in the Red Sea for his people and fed them in a wondrous manner in the desert, so he may have mercy on us in our danger. I believe that, if our faith does not waver, He will not allow us to remain fasting today, a day which he has illuminated with so many wondrous tokens of his majesty.   (Colgrave, *Two Lives of Cuthbert*, pp. 193–4)

Cuthbert then led them to the beach where he had been praying and there they found three pieces of dolphin meat cut and prepared to cook. Cuthbert told them that the three pieces represented the three days they would be stuck where they were. And this is how it turned out, for on the third day the sea became calm and they were able to return to base.

When Cuthbert was about thirty, Eata, the abbot and bishop of Lindisfarne, invited him to become prior of the Island. Cuthbert's task was to help the brothers who had not left for Iona and Ireland to convert to the practices of the Roman Church. There were still brethren present who were doubtful about losing their own traditions and ways, but Cuthbert persuaded them there was much to gain by being a united Church and that the links with Rome could be enriching. There is no doubt that his own devotion and dedication were an inspiration.

In addition to his demanding duties on the Island, we are told Cuthbert also visited people on the mainland to encourage them in the faith, and he is credited with miracles of healing through his prayer, his touch and through exorcism. As often as possible, he would escape to pray and sing psalms on little Hobthrush Island, but even here his devotions were invaded. He needed more time in solitude, to be alone with God.

In 676, after 12 years in office, Cuthbert obtained permission from his friend Eata to cease being prior and to withdraw to the island of Inner Farne, where Aidan had gone sometimes before him, to spend time in solitude and unbroken prayer. Bede writes:

> Now after he had completed many years in the same monastery, he joyfully entered into the remote solitudes which he had long desired, sought and prayed for, with the good will of that same abbot and also the brethren. He rejoiced because, after a long and blameless active life, he was now counted worthy to rise to the repose of divine contemplation.
>
> (Colgrave, *Two Lives of Cuthbert*, p. 215)

Cuthbert recognized the need for rhythm in life. Like tidal Holy Island, we sometimes need to be part of the mainland and all that is going on, and sometimes need to separate out and be an island for a while. Perpetual busyness is a great danger to the life of the spirit, and in our modern world of constant noise and activity it is more important than ever to learn to be alone with God.

Cuthbert sought to grow his own food and raised a crop of barley, though he had to stop the birds from consuming it all.

It is also said he reprimanded them for stealing thatch from the roof of his house, though when the birds left he felt very guilty for chasing away part of God's creation and prayed they would return. Happily they did, one bringing a large piece of fat in its beak, which Cuthbert accepted as a gift and used to waterproof his boots! This must have been the time when he developed his love for the eider duck, which still makes its nest at the very door of the little chapel on Inner Farne.

Though Inner Farne is over a mile off the coast and far more difficult to reach than Hobthrush Island, people came in great numbers to see Cuthbert, many attracted by stories of his miracles. He even had a guest house built where they could stay. Bede tells us: 'No one went away from him without enjoying his consolation, and no one returned accompanied by that sorrow of mind which had brought him hither' (Colgrave, *Two Lives of Cuthbert*, p. 229). Cuthbert planned to spend the rest of his life on this little island, but the Church in its wisdom thought differently. At a synod held in 684, probably at nearby Alnmouth, attended by Archbishop Theodore, Bishop Trumwine and King Egfrith, it was decided that Cuthbert should be the next bishop of Hexham. Messengers were sent to Cuthbert, but it was not until the king himself, accompanied by Bishop Trumwine and brethren from Lindisfarne, came to his hermitage, that he assented. He came to the synod in tears, loath to leave his island home.

On Easter Day 685, Cuthbert was consecrated bishop of Hexham by Archbishop Theodore in York. Almost immediately he and Eata exchanged dioceses, and Cuthbert became bishop of Lindisfarne. For nearly two years, he acted as a statesman and saw to the consecration of churches and the ordination of priests. He cared for and visited his people, from Carlisle in the west, to Crayke outside York, where he had been given a villa. Spending much time travelling around and nurturing newly formed monasteries and churches, he was seen by many as a visionary, a prophet and a healer.

Cuthbert was now 52 years old, a good age for any man of his times, and the great demands that hard work and travelling had made upon his life had taken a physical toll. He felt it was time to lay down his episcopal oversight and prepare to meet his God. And so, when the Christmas celebrations of 686 were over, Cuthbert resigned his see and left Lindisfarne for Inner Farne and his hermitage. As the brethren watched the frail figure get into a boat, one aged monk asked, 'Tell us my Lord Bishop, when may we hope for your return?'

Aware that the end was near, Cuthbert replied, 'When you bring my body back here.' This caused a good deal of alarm but Cuthbert made little of it, and set sail with a joyous heart. He felt as if he were returning home. At last he would have time to enjoy the presence and love of God without too many duties and disturbances.

Cuthbert hoped to be buried on Inner Farne but very reluctantly assented to the monks' wish for his body to be brought back to Lindisfarne. He warned them:

> It was my desire that my body should rest here where, to some extent, I have fought my fight for the Lord, where I desire to finish my course, and where I shall hope to be raised up to receive the crown of righteousness from the righteous judge. But I also think it would be more expedient for you that I should remain here, on account of the influx of fugitives and guilty men of every sort who will flee to my body . . . and you will be compelled very frequently to intercede with the powers of the world . . . If you wish to set aside my plans and take my body back there, it seems best that you entomb it in the interior of your church, so that while you yourselves can visit my sepulchre when you wish, it may be in your power to decide whether any of those who come thither should approach it.   (Colgrave, *Two Lives of Cuthbert*, p. 279)

On 20 March 687, two burning torches lit by a monk on Inner Farne told the brethren on Lindisfarne that Cuthbert had died. His body was brought over the water, placed in a stone sarcophagus, and buried on the right hand side of the altar in the church now dedicated to St Peter. Almost immediately, miracles were recorded at Cuthbert's tomb and pilgrims flocked to be near where the holy man was buried. Eleven years after Cuthbert's death, it was decided to elevate his body, which involved digging up his mortal remains, washing the bones and placing them in a position in which they might be seen and venerated. Imagine everyone's amazement when the sarcophagus was opened and they found Cuthbert's body still intact! He looked as if he was just sleeping. Cuthbert's shrine became one of the most visited in Europe, and the gifts borne by pilgrims made the church among the richest in the land.

As Aidan helped unite British and Angles, so Cuthbert, through modelling a life on holiness and devotion, helped bring unity to the Church in the North.

Before I left Cuthbert's Island, I thought back to that strange day in 1993, when I had celebrated communion there. It was 20 March, the anniversary of Cuthbert's death. The day was clear and there was hardly a breath of wind, but as I asked the congregation to keep silence and give thanks for Cuthbert, a great cloud of smoke arose from Inner Farne to the south of us. Higher and higher it climbed before dispersing. It is very rare to see smoke coming from Inner Farne, and the experience only served to deepen our thanksgiving for Cuthbert.

imago aequilae

The Golden Age of Northumbria

An enemy ended my life, deprived me
of my physical strength; then he dipped me
in water and drew me out again,
and put me in the sun where I soon shed
all my hair. After that, the knife's sharp edge
bit into me, and all my blemishes were scraped away.
Fingers folded me, and a bird's feather
often moved over my brown surface,
sprinkling meaningful marks; it swallowed more wood-dye
(part of the stream) and again travelled over me,
leaving black tracks. Then a man bound me,
he stretched skin over me and adorned me
with gold; thus I am enriched by wondrous work
of smiths, wound round with metal . . .
. . . Ask what I am called,
of such use to men. My name is famous,
of service to men and sacred in itself.

> (Kevin Crossley-Holland, *The Anglo-Saxon World:
> An Anthology*, Oxford University Press, 1984, p. 241)

On a hot summer's day, surrounded by about twenty-five children, it was a joy to walk the Pilgrim's Way that links Lindisfarne and the mainland. As we ambled along, we picked up feathers – goose or swan wing feathers if we could find them – until we had enough to make a quill pen for each child. We were going to pretend to be scribes and, at the same time, discover how a bird's feather was used to produce one of the greatest pieces of art ever created.

After the Synod of Whitby things changed rapidly. Growing unity and the spread of the faith across various small kingdoms ushered in what has been described as the 'Golden Age' of the Church in Northumbria. Under Wilfrid's supervision, great churches were built in stone: the one at Hexham was said to be the finest this side of the Alps. Ripon was also given a grand church, as was York, Wilfrid's episcopal seat. These impressive structures, which towered above the wooden buildings around them, were a sign of how well endowed and wealthy the Church was becoming. Without prosperity and relative peace, the creating of fine buildings would not have been possible.

Much is due to the generosity of the kings of this period. Benedict Biscop, who accompanied Wilfrid on his first journey to Italy, was given 70 hides of land by king Egfrith to build his monastic foundation at Wearmouth, and some years later another 40 hides of land on the south bank of the Tyne at Jarrow to erect a second monastery. Benedict Biscop deliberately chose to build in 'the Roman Style' and imported stonemasons and glaziers from Gaul. The dedication stone at Jarrow records the date of this second foundation as 685, the same year that St Cuthbert was made bishop. Smaller churches were also built, like that at Escomb in county Durham. Though there is no trace of a stone church on Holy Island for this period, it is interesting to note that there are Saxon quoin stones to be seen in the present church of St Mary's. We do know that Eadbert, Cuthbert's successor as bishop of Lindisfarne, had the thatch on the wooden church of St Peter on the island removed, and the roof and walls covered with lead. Not only would this have been an expensive process, the result must have looked somewhat strange.

As building work progressed, the arts also prospered. The cross-fertilizing of Celtic, secular Anglo-Saxon and continental Christian influences produced some of Northumbria's finest art: carved stonework; woodwork, as in the series of figures incised on the oak of Cuthbert's coffin; Franks Casket (a small chest carved out of whale bone and now housed in the British Museum); and, of course, the Lindisfarne Gospels. When I was presented with a facsimile of the Gospels on becoming vicar of

Holy Island, I felt overwhelmed by the treasure I held in my hand: what wonders there are between its pages!

It is believed that the script and art work of the Gospels are the work of Eadfrith, the first English artist we know by name, indeed the 'father of English art', though no one has ever been able to trace his place of birth, his family, or where he got his early training as a scribe. Eadfrith became bishop of Lindisfarne around 698, and until recently it was believed he completed the Gospels prior to this appointment. However, the present Curator of Manuscripts at the British Library, Michelle P. Brown, believes there is a case to be made for a later date of between 715 and 720 for their creation, near the end of Eadfrith's life in 721.

The Lindisfarne Gospels would have taken a minimum of two years to complete, and possibly a good deal longer. A note at the end of the volume, written by the priest Aldred at Chester-le-Street in County Durham over 250 years after the Gospels were created, states simply:

> Eadfrith, Bishop of the Lindisfarne Church, originally wrote this book, for God and for Saint Cuthbert and, jointly, for the saints whose relics are in the Island. And Ethelwald, Bishop of the Lindisfarne islanders, impressed it on the outside and covered it, as he well knew how to do. And Billfrith, the hermit, forged the ornaments which are on it on the outside and adorned it with gold and with gems and also with silver-gilt – pure metal. And Aldred, unworthy and most miserable priest, glossed it in English between the lines with the help of God and Saint Cuthbert.

When speaking to children's groups about the Lindisfarne Gospels, I would ask a number of questions. First, what would have been needed to create them? Most obviously, a Bible to copy from. The text is in Latin, the Vulgate version created largely by the labours of Jerome and subsequently adopted throughout all of Europe, and the list of festivals recorded at the front of the Gospels suggests Eadfrith's copy of the Bible may have originated in Naples. It may possibly have been brought from a nearby monastery by Hadrian, Archbishop Theodore's assistant, and given to the church on Lindisfarne on its rededication in the name of St Peter.

To get the children thinking further, I would ask them to look at the riddle that opens this chapter. When they had worked out that it was about the making of a book, I would ask, 'And how would you like to have to shave a page before you write on it?'

For the Gospels are written on calf skin. Each skin would measure slightly more than two feet wide and be about fifteen inches in depth. Examination of the pages has revealed that the spines of the animals ran horizontally, so when a skin was folded once, it would create four pages. Every four skins are made into a gathering of 16 pages. As the Gospels are 516 pages long, at least 129 unblemished skins would be required. This gives us an insight into the planning and preparation involved in creating such a book: a period of stability would be necessary so farms could rear the creatures; a whole team of people would then need to care for the cattle and prepare the calf skin for use; another group would have to resource and prepare some of the pigments for the illustrations, and it is interesting that the dominant colours are those of the island itself – pinks, purples, greens and deep blue.

Once four sheets had been folded to make a group of 16 pages, the top page was measured out for writing in two columns of 25 to 26 lines each. Eadfrith chose to write in the formal Insular Majuscule Script which originated in Ireland and became a speciality of the British Isles. His ink was made from lamp black (the soot from candle flames) mixed with egg white. Indeed, egg white was the fixative used almost throughout the Gospels. I tell the children I can recommend it as a glue, for it has lasted for almost thirteen hundred years.

There are 15 elaborately decorated pages. The first major page is the beginning of St Jerome's letter to Pope Damasus, with its opening words, *Novum opus facere me cogis ex veteri* –

'Out of something old, you have compelled me to make something new.' Now there was challenge if ever there was one! Not a new gospel but a fresh presentation of the gospel. This is what Aidan and Cuthbert had managed so effectively and this, I would tell the children, is what I was called to do on Lindisfarne – and they are called to do in their lives.

If you look at these opening words you will see they are decorated with many birds, like so much of the manuscript, but then one might expect this from a calligrapher living on a small island.

Each Gospel has a page on which the evangelists are depicted as real people, this being the first book we know of in the British Isles to show them this way and not just by their symbols. The image of St John facing the reader with his hand over his heart, as he appears on St Cuthbert's coffin, is unique to British and Irish art.

There are five pages of intricate interweaving, reminiscent of eastern carpets, based around a cross shape. One of these introduces St Jerome's letter (see above), and the other four precede the opening page of each Gospel. The cross on the carpet page of St Matthew is probably the best known in the Gospels. It is made up not only of many birds but of five chalices each having a circular host. As the bread is broken during communion, so these hosts depict the five wounds of Christ. The same five wounds are found on Cuthbert's portable altar in the shape of crosses.

In the decorated initial page at the beginning of St Luke's Gospel, the artist has used over ten thousand red dots to make a pattern, while on St Mark's carpet page, it has been calculated that there are more than seven thousand intersections without one mistake. Some suggest, however, that Eadfrith may have introduced a few deliberate errors in his art work to remind us that only God is perfect.

The Gospels are vividly coloured. For the red, Eadfrith used either kermes, obtained from insects living in the evergreen oaks of the Mediterranean area, or red lead. The indigo appears to be either of Oriental origin or from woad belonging to northern Europe. The pinks and purples would have come from a range of flowers, plants and sea creatures. The most exciting material of all, lapis lazuli, provides the deep blue.

Being in the sea, the island was on the main trading routes of its day, and not nearly as remote as we might imagine. Did the scribe purposely collect his colours from all the known world to show that the Gospels represent the whole united Church, at one in its proclamation of the 'old story of the Good News'?

Once all the written and art work was completed, Ethelwald, who would become bishop of Lindisfarne on the death of Eadfrith, covered and bound the book together. Sadly this binding has long disappeared. (The oldest European binding still in existence is a copy of the Gospel of St John which once belonged to St Cuthbert and was made at Monkwearmouth/ Jarrow.) As a young man in the monastery, Ethelwald had assisted Cuthbert and had been present at a miracle of Cuthbert's when he cured a kinswoman of pains in her head and down one side of her body. Soon after the elevation of St Cuthbert, Ethelwald was made the prior of Melrose and then its abbot, before coming to Lindisfarne on Eadfrith's death. Ethelwald himself died in 740 and was buried at the foot of a large stone cross that he had erected on Lindisfarne. The base of this cross is possibly the one found between St Mary's church and the priory. The cross itself was possibly destroyed in one of the Viking invasions.

We know nothing of Billfrith, also mentioned by Aldred, except that he was a hermit and that he decorated the cover of the book using precious gems, gold and silver gilt. The silver plates on the portable altar among the Cuthbert relics are thought to be contemporary and so show what Billfrith's workmanship would have been like.

From the very beginning, the Lindisfarne Gospels were regarded as very precious, and used only on special occasions. They showed the devotion of their creator to the Gospels and his ability to take time and meditate with a quill and paints in his hand. This is not a book you can rush – you are meant to pore over its pages and contemplate its word; to spend time exploring its depth and mystery. In the Lindisfarne Gospels we discover that all of creation is interwoven in the love of God, which seeks a response from the heart.

———◆———

After the children had gone, I looked again at the facsimile in St Mary's, and was reminded that every time I celebrated communion, I walked on a carpet page. For the island women, under the guidance of Kathleen Parbury, who created the St Aidan statue and sculpted the font cover, made a carpet for the sanctuary based on the St Mark's carpet page from the Lindisfarne Gospels. And when I go to the Fishermen's Altar and stand next to the tiny wicker coracle (in which I have actually sailed to Cuthbert's island), I am on a similar, though smaller, carpet, made by the island women for the year 2000 and designed by Jean Freer who lives in North Yorkshire. The influence of Eadfrith's art continues down the centuries. And standing on one of the carpets is as good a place as any to give thanks for all who have contributed to enriching the island in any way.

The Fury of the Norsemen

How all must lament this day,
When the pagan troop,
Coming from the ends of the earth,
Suddenly sought our shores by ship.
Despoiling our fathers' venerable tombs of their splendour.
(Alcuin, 'On the Destruction of the Monastery
of Lindisfarne', eighth century)

I could hear the skylarks singing as I stood on the lonely north shore of Lindisfarne. Before me terns chattered away as they dived for food, and on the far horizon a ship was coming into view. The world seemed quite idyllic . . . But suddenly a cloud covered the sun, and out of nowhere, there appeared two Arctic skua, who scattered the terns and continued to chase a few until they had disgorged their food. The display of skill and persistence was admirable, though the skua were behaving just like pirates in the way they attacked and took what they could. Indeed, the ship on the horizon now began to look dark and rather threatening! In a moment I was back in 793, one of the most difficult years on this seemingly idyllic island. The Anglo-Saxon Chronicle relates events in dramatic fashion:

> Ann. DCC.XCIII: – In this year dire forewarnings came over the land of the Northumbrians, and miserably terrified the people: these were extraordinary whirlwinds and lightning and fiery dragons were seen flying in the air. A great famine followed soon upon these omens; and soon after that in that same year, on the 6th of the ides of Ianr, the havoc of the heathen men miserably destroyed God's church on Lindisfarne through rapine and slaughter.

In the Latin calendar the ides was accounted as the thirteenth day of all months except March, May, July and October when it was the fifteenth day. Thus the sixth day before the ides of January would be the 8th. However, while it is quite possible the sea raid was made in winter, it is not very likely. Simeon of Durham, the twelfth-century chronicler who used Northumbrian sources to write his *History of the Church of Durham*, gives a different date in his account of the destruction of the monastic settlement:

> In the year from the incarnation of our Lord seven hundred and ninety three – being the hundred and seventh year from the death of father Cuthbert, and the eleventh of the pontificate of Higbald, and the fifth of the reign of that most wicked king Aethelred – the church of Lindisfarne was miserably filled with devastation, blood and rapine, and all but entirely and thoroughly ruined . . . Its approaching destruction, and that of other holy places, was presaged by the appearance of fearful thunders and fiery dragons flying through the sky. Presently after this, and in the same year, a fleet of the pagans arrived in Britain from the north; and rushing hither and thither, and plundering as they went, they slew not only the cattle, but even the priests and deacons, and the choirs of monks and nuns. On the seventh of the ides of June, they reached the church of Lindisfarne, and there they miserably ravaged and pillaged everything; they trod the holy things under polluted feet, they dug down the altars, and plundered all the treasures of the church. Some of the brethren they slew, some they carried off with them in chains, the greater number they stripped naked, insulted, and cast out of doors, and some they drowned in the sea.

Simeon's dating of the destruction of Lindisfarne as 'the seventh of the ides of June' (7 June) is accepted by the majority of scholars as the more likely, and it is thought that the date in the Anglo-Saxon Chronicle was due to a scribal error. I happened to be on the island in 1993 when this June date was kept in commemoration of the event 12 centuries before. We had many Norwegians coming to the island on pilgrimage during the year, and a Viking longboat rowed into the harbour, but it only came from Berwick harbour under supervision and some of its rowers were seasick on arrival!

Simeon's account suggests that the invaders were concerned with ravaging a wider area than just Lindisfarne, but the raid on 7 June 973 clearly targeted the island. Due to the many pilgrims who came bearing gifts, the shrine was rich indeed, quite unlike in the days of Aidan. It is just possible that the Vikings had done their homework and knew there were great treasures and only monks to defend them. It would be far easier to attack Lindisfarne than a fortress like Bamburgh.

In the event, some monks were killed or driven into the sea to drown, while others were taken as slaves and quite possibly became the first missionaries in the land of their captors. The treasures of the shrine were stolen, though for some strange reason Cuthbert, the Lindisfarne Gospels and many relics were left untouched. It could be that the islanders quickly hid some treasures and that Cuthbert's wooden coffin did not seem a likely trophy.

That such a holy place could be despoiled sent shock waves throughout Europe. It was an attack not only on the body but on the spirit of the country. Alcuin, who descended from a noble Northumbrian family and had been the Master of the Cathedral School in York, was an adviser to the Frankish court of Charlemagne at the time of the Viking invasion. Writing to king Aethelred of Northumbria he reveals his horror at what has happened:

Lo it is nearly 350 years that we and our fathers have inhabited this most lovely land, and never before has such terror appeared in Britain as we have now suffered from a pagan race, nor was it thought possible that such an inroad from the sea could be made.

Behold the church of St Cuthbert spattered with the blood of the priests of God, despoiled of its ornaments; a place more venerable than in all Britain is given as prey to pagan people.

And where first, after the departure of Saint Paulinus from York, the Christian religion in our race took its rise, there misery and calamity have begun. Who does not fear this? Who does not lament this as if his country was captured?

(John Marsden, *The Fury of the Northmen*, Book Club Associates, 1993, p. 34)

In another letter to Bishop Higbald of Lindisfarne, Alcuin offers to do what he can to obtain the liberty of any who have been taken away as slaves. This would be achieved either through payment in gold or by exchanging other hostages:

When our lord King Charles returns home, having by the mercy of God subdued his enemies, we plan, with God's help, to go to him; and if we can be any profit to your Holiness, regarding either the youths who have been led into captivity by the pagans or any other of your needs, we will take diligent care to bring it about. (Marsden, *The Fury*, p. 45)

That Alcuin was able to write to Higbald shows that the bishop was among the survivors. Though the loss of treasures may have been great, there is no doubt the community survived with enough members. Simeon says:

Although the church of Lindisfarne had been thus ravaged and despoiled of its ecclesiastical ornaments, the episcopal see still continued therein; and as many of the monks had succeeded in escaping from the hands of the barbarians still continued for a long time to reside near the body of the blessed Cuthbert. (Marsden, *The Fury*, p. 39)

Alcuin, aware of this new danger, wrote a letter to Wearmouth and Jarrow in 793 saying: 'Consider whom you have as your defence against the pagans who have appeared on your coast.' The capture of slaves and the taking of treasure obviously whetted the appetite of the great seamen, whose oak longboats carried carvings of fierce beasts like dragons on their prows. In 794, Monkwearmouth/Jarrow was only one of many places raided; in 795 both Iona and Inisboffin were devastated, and by the 830s whole fleets of Danes were invading cities as well as monastic settlements. During this period the fourteenth bishop of Lindisfarne, Ecgred, had one of the church buildings moved to Norham, feeling it would be safer to be away from the sea. However, it was not until 875, when the Danes raided Tynemouth Priory and destroyed it, that the sixteenth bishop, Eardulph, decided it was time for the monks to leave the island and seek a safe home for the body of Cuthbert and other relics, including the head of Oswald and some of the bones of Aidan. Simeon of Durham, describing the 'Cuthbert Congregation' as they became known, says, 'They wandered throughout the whole district of Northumbria, having no settled dwelling place; they were like sheep flying before wolves.'

After travelling around northern England and the south-west corner of Scotland, the monks rested at Norham on the banks of the Tweed before finally coming to settle at Chester-le-Street in County Durham. They were there for over a hundred years and then yet another Danish scare forced them to move. They got as far as Ripon in North Yorkshire and then turned back northwards. Finally in 995 they came to Durham, and there a Saxon church was built and Cuthbert's relics translated to it in 999.

The Viking invasions brought to an end the Golden Age of Northumbria, and, for the island too, it was the end of an era. Eardulph would be the last bishop of Lindisfarne. Under the Vikings, wealth was redistributed, landed estates taken over, and the economic strength of the Church weakened. The creation of books was disrupted by the loss of grazing land and thus the availability of animal skins, while the making of church plate and high-quality artefacts all needed a settled environment, with a ready supply of teachers and equipment. For a while this was gone.

As I felt for the terns being harassed by the skua, I thought of those today whose lands and homes are being invaded, whose lives are filled with terror and darkness. There are many still oppressed and robbed of well-being in our world.

'From the fury of evil men, good Lord, deliver us.'

Island Church and Priory

In Saxon strength the abbey frown'd.
With massive arches broad and round.
That rose alternate, row and row,
On ponderous columns short and low,
Built ere the art was known,
By pointed aisle, and shafted stalk,
The arcades of an alley'd walk
To emulate in stone.
(Walter Scott, *Marmion*, p. 40)

I watched with great fascination as Cuthbert came to the island. He seemed to be shrouded in grave clothes (or, as one fisherman remarked, done up like a salmon!). His journey down the street towards the parish church was extremely slow. Then for a while he lay totally still – before being lifted unceremoniously from his resting place (a low loader) by the prongs of a forklift truck. For this was no spirit, but a larger-than-life-size statue of Cuthbert being transported to the priory to be placed in the outer court. A greened bronze by the English sculptor Fenwick Lawson, it portrays the stillness and power of Cuthbert: he sits quietly, with folded hands and an eider duck at his feet.

Though the castle has become the iconic image of Lindisfarne, the ruined priory is possibly the most romantic building on the island. It is worth taking time to see how the wind and rain have carved many of the priory stones into wonderful shapes, and reduced some of the original round pillars at the great west door to straight slabs.

Many assume that the ruination of the building was caused by the Vikings, but it is only poetic licence that allows Sir Walter Scott to associate the present priory with the events of the eighth to tenth centuries: in fact, it dates from the early part of the twelfth. The rebuilding of the priory came about because the Benedictines wished to establish a monastic site on the island, and to cater once more for the pilgrims coming to see where the saints had lived and worked.

On the departure of the Cuthbert Congregation in 875 it is not known if the island was left totally uninhabited. If so, it would not be for long: a place so special to the hearts of Northumbrians – and so richly resourced in terms of fishing and farming – would still have the power to draw. Yet for more than two centuries we know little of what happened on the island. Saxon farm dwellings have been discovered among the dunes near the North Shore, and a collection of Anglo-Saxon stone carvings, dating from the eighth to the tenth centuries, is housed in the Priory Museum. These include name stones, fragments of cross shafts, and what is known as the 'battle stone', which has carvings of warriors on one side and, on the other, two hands upholding the symbol of the cross, with two figures kneeling below it, and the sun and moon above.

In the winter of 1069–70, three years on from the Battle of Hastings when he and his band of Normans had famously defeated King Harold II and the English army, William the Conqueror had already advanced as far north as York. The last Anglo-Saxon bishop of Durham, Ethelwine, and his monks, fearing the wrath of the new king, left the city and set off for Lindisfarne. With them they carried Cuthbert's body and other relics. The first night of their journey was spent at Jarrow, the second at Bedlington in Northumberland and the third at Tughall. On the fourth day, as they wearily approached Lindisfarne, they found the tide was in. Just as some of the elderly monks were beginning to tremble at the thought of having to spend a dark and stormy night without shelter, the sea suddenly seemed to open before them. They were able to cross over to the island, and everyone rejoiced at this apparently miraculous event (though we might suspect they did not know about the tides, and this was simply the natural daily tide change).

As the priory had been ruined by the Vikings, it is likely that Cuthbert's body and the other relics, including the Lindisfarne

Gospels, were kept in the church of St Mary the Virgin. By Lent 1070, Ethelwine had decided to leave England with the holy relics and join William the Conqueror's enemies in France. However, the wintry weather prevented him setting off by ship at Wearmouth, and he was taken captive by the Normans and put in prison. Cuthbert and his relics were taken back to Durham that spring. Never again would they be restored to the island, but Cuthbert was yet to pay a visit . . .

In 1082 the Cuthbert Congregation at Durham, who traced their descent to those who had left Lindisfarne at the time of the Viking raids, were told they must become monks in the Benedictine monastery or leave. The treasures, together with most of their extensive land holdings, were transferred to the Benedictines and the cathedral of Durham. William of Calais, the bishop of Durham, gave 'the church at Lindisfarne, which had originally been an episcopal see, with its adjacent vill of Fenham, and the church at Norham, which had been rendered illustrious by the body of St Cuthbert, with its vill of Shoreswood' to the Benedictines. Within two years the island had become known as 'Holy Island' in honour of the saints who had lived and died there, though it remained in a subordinate position, as a priory belonging to Durham and the Benedictines. The mother church had become the daughter.

The building of a new priory church on the island began in about 1122 and must have been completed by 1150 at the latest. The stone used came from Cheswick on the mainland, as that on the island was not thought to be suitable. People from all around the district helped cart the stone on wains and wagons, and it was said that many were so pleased to help they gave their labour and transport for free. Considering the difficulties involved, this only confirms the love the locals had for the island and its saints: a wagon bogged down with the tide coming in would be no joke!

When completed, the priory would be dedicated to St Peter, as the former priory had been by Archbishop Theodore. However, a monk named Reginald of Durham, in one of the very few 'ghost stories' of the island, describes a miraculous appearance by Cuthbert at its consecration. In the early morning light, before the day's activities began, he was seen coming out of the 'old church', that is, St Mary's (which would have been used for worship in the meantime), and processing with other vested priests and monks of old into the new building. There Cuthbert celebrated Mass to dedicate the priory, before the ghostly procession returned to the old church, went inside to divest and duly disappeared. Whatever you make of this story it tells us that there were two churches in existence, standing in line, as they do today.

The parish church is in fact the oldest building in use on the island, and the only one with any work from the Saxon period. In the wall that divides the nave from the chancel there is a little Saxon arch above the more modern Early English one. High above this is a typical Saxon 'door'. On the outside of the building, you can see Saxon quoin stones where the nave joins the chancel. We shall never know for sure, but some of these now much worn Saxon stones may just be those that were used to surround Aidan's wooden church. There could have been a church on this site since 635.

The twelfth-century Norman work carried out in St Mary's was intended to extend or reorder the building, and it would seem this was undertaken around the time the priory was built, the chance to use the stonemasons employed there being too good to miss. And so the north side of the church got its three rounded Norman arches, with their pleasing alternation of red and white stone – the only example of this style to be found in Northumberland. Later the priory church was given an Early English extension at its east end, and it is likely this building work was done at the same time as St Mary's was given an aisle and its southern arches – these being the pointed arches, including the small one to the back of the north side of the church, and the chancel arch. The chancel, with its three very beautiful long lancet windows, is also Early English. The main shape of the church as we see it today was completed in the thirteenth century.

There are various memorials in St Mary's, the oldest, which is likely to be from the twelfth century, is inset into the north wall of the chancel and appears to be a mitre and a cross, with a sword. Under the chancel arch on the south side is a memorial to Sir William Reed of Fenham, one time governor of the castle who died in 1604. On it is the inscription *Contra vim mortis non est medicamen in hortis*, which translates, 'Against the power of death there is no remedy in the garden', though I hope Sir William would see a remedy in the Easter garden. While the priory has always attracted pilgrims and visitors, the smaller St Mary's has faithfully served as the parish church. There has been some benefit in being the poorer relative: when in the sixteenth century Henry VIII ordered the dissolution of the monasteries, the priory suffered ruination, but the church survived because it served the local parish rather than the monks.

The priory church of St Peter, though relatively small in size for a priory church, was given an architectural design of a grand order. It had the normal cruciform plan, with an aisled nave, an aisleless chancel and transepts. The chancel and transepts each originally had a rounded apse, and each apse was likely to contain an altar for the daily celebration by the ordained monks. The aisled nave had six bays, though the north and south aisles are very narrow. The church's most striking feature was the high central tower over the transept crossing. One of the two stone ribs that supported the central tower still stands and it is known by all as 'The Rainbow Arch'. Before health and safety and the careful eye of English Heritage, island lads used to walk across this arch as a dare! Many of the features of the priory church are in the Norman style and copied from Durham Cathedral: the west front with its stair turrets has a grand Norman door with dog-tooth patterning, and the pillars of the arches on the north side, which remain to this day, have zig-zag and diaper fluting as at Durham. In the latter part of the twelfth century, the priory must have been thriving, for the chancel apse was demolished and the chancel doubled in length and given a squared east end.

However, there was no going back to the grand days of the Celts, with a place for teaching and a scriptorium. Certainly in the early days of the new priory, there would only be five or six Benedictines to maintain the daily services, care for the pilgrims and islanders and run the estate: the endowments of the parish, which provided its income, were the island itself, including the manors of Fenham and Shoreswood, and various farms on the mainland. The account books of the fourteenth century show a small group of monks busy brewing and baking, fishing and farming, as you would expect. But they were also involved in organizing coal-mining, quarrying and lime-burning as well as trading in seaweed and iron. Much of their work set a pattern for the people of the island, and fishing, farming and lime-burning became the main occupations. Fishermen were employed to work the priory boats, while others farmed its land, growing corn, beans, onions, and hay for the cattle and horses. Hemp and flax were also produced and the monks were involved in the making and selling of cloth. Women got the job of milking the sheep! With such local involvement, many people were assured of a livelihood.

We know that in 1325 the priory received £160 in tithes and £56 in land rents. Its account books begin the following year, and continue up to its dissolution in 1537. They give a wonderful glimpse into the way the monks lived, and for their times they lived very well. The year 1326, however, was a year of disaster, due to the Scottish army, which had been defeated at Bannockburn in 1314, making destructive border raids. The priory itself suffered only one minor attack in 1326, when the brewhouse and bakehouse were looted (after all, Aidan and Cuthbert would be regarded by the raiders as fellow Scots), but its income dropped to only £15 from tithes and £17 from land rents, due to the devastation wrought by raiders on the mainland. In 1328 Tweedmouth, Holburn, Lowick, Barmoor, Bowsden, Ancroft, Cheswick, Scremerston, Kyloe and Orde were laid waste and could contribute nothing. The income that year was only £69 – including £20 from wool tithes, £8 from Tweedmouth fishing and £8 from Holy Island parish church and its chapelries – a far cry from the £200 of 1325. Durham Cathedral, displeased that its share of income was so reduced, appointed Gilbert of Elwick to manage the priory affairs. This seems to have been effective, for in 1330 the income went up to £173. However, this was offset by an unusual number of sheep dying, and, after expenses, the priory only broke about even. In 1348, when the great pandemic known as the Black Death decimated the population, the income from tithes dropped dramatically, and it would never again rise to the level of the early part of the century.

Most of the time it would seem there was a prior and five monks who were assisted by seven esquires and 13 servants. That the monks were more gentlemen than peasants seems to be confirmed by the fact that in 1346–47 they consumed 36 stone of cheese, 48 suckling pigs, 92 geese, 80 hens, 2 pigs, 15 oxen, 73 sheep, 2 lampreys, codfish, 150 herring, 6 salted salmon and other whitefish in abundance. They also had $2^1/_2$ lbs of draget (a sugar cake eaten at festivals), $^1/_2$ lb lump sugar, $2^1/_2$ lbs of white sugar and 8 lbs of black sugar, plus $^1/_4$ lb of cloves, $^1/_2$ lb white pepper and other spices in abundance. This was rich fare indeed.

Like many other northern monasteries, Holy Island was fortified in the early fourteenth century, and traces of these fortifications can be seen along the walls of the outer court with its parapet, walk and battlements. The church was given battle-mented parapets and, in the west gable, loop-holes for the firing of arrows were added. In the inventories for the time there are mentions of various pieces of armour, weapons and gun-powder. However, following the renewal of the Anglo-Scottish war in 1384, the priory petitioned the Crown for permission not to fortify the priory, fearing perhaps that fortifications would only antagonize any invaders: it was in a particularly vulnerable position, being easily looked down on from the Heugh, and those it housed would have been able to offer only poor resistance. The petition being successful, the priory was not attacked like its sister houses at Coldingham and on Inner Farne, and monks from these places came to Lindisfarne for refuge, along with some of the local clergy who stayed as paying guests. The priory's finances were so low due to the war that paying guests would no doubt have been warmly welcomed; in 1385–86, a collection box was put at the door of the church to help meet costs.

The year 1537 saw the beginning of a new chapter for the priory, while bringing to an end the monastic occupation which had endured for nine hundred years. The fifty-ninth and last prior of Lindisfarne, Thomas Sparke, was pensioned off as a suffragan bishop of Berwick. Soon stone from the priory was being used to help build the castle on Beblow Crag (of which more shortly), and 1613 saw the priory's despoilment, when Lord Walden, Earl of Dunbar, took the lead from its roof, its bells and anything else of value. His heavily laden ship sailed out of the harbour and soon afterwards sank in a storm: local fishermen say they think they know where the lead lies on the seabed.

Once opened to the elements the priory went into decay, and by 1820 most of the nave and the central tower had crumbled and collapsed. Around this time the Selby family, as lords of the manor, sought to clear away debris and to set upon some repair. They did not manage to prevent the west front tumbling down in 1850, but the Crown paid for it to be rebuilt. Today the priory is under the care of English Heritage and one of its busiest sites. Each year pilgrims come in their thousands to visit or worship within the grounds.

We processed in and stood before the bronze cast of Cuthbert in the outer courtyard of the priory: the local Anglican and Roman Catholic bishops, a good number of clergy, Fenwick Lawson the sculptor, and many lay people and school children. I wondered why Cuthbert had been relegated to outside the priory church rather than inside, near where he was believed to have been buried, but could find no answer. Indeed, if I were Reginald of Durham, I might have wondered if Cuthbert had come the night before and seen to the dedication!

The Castle and Some Characters

The great Commander of the Gormorants,
The Geese and Ganders of these Hallowed Lands,
Where Lindisfarne and Holy Iland stands,
These worthless lines sends to yo' worthie hands.
(Captain Rugg, 1643)

It was a cold Easter Monday. I watched a fulmar near the castle as it caught the wind and moved without apparent effort. Until last century there were few documented fulmars in all of England, but now this 'invader' is totally at home in the local quarries as well as at Bamburgh and Holy Island castles. I was taking a small group of children to see where the birds nested. Suddenly there was a great commotion in front of me. Two young lads were fighting over a 'treasure' washed up on the beach. It was something of little worth but they were both determined to have it. My mind went back to another battle for possession on the same spot, one Easter long ago. It is a story of storm, shipwreck and hospitality.

A mysterious man whose real name was Gilbert Blakhal embarked on a voyage from Dieppe to Leith, near Edinburgh, on 1 April 1643. Mr Blakhal was in truth a Roman Catholic priest and a Jesuit, and thus subject to harassment and persecution in seventeenth-century Britain. If anyone asked, 'What is your name, sir?' he would answer, 'Ross, Ross is my name', turn up the collar of his cloak, and resume his habitual watch over the darkening ocean. After four relatively calm days, the sea grew choppy. Snow fell like a grey mist, obliterating everything in sight. A storm blew up out of the north and the waves became mountainous. The ship was lashed on every side, and Ross feared that this might be the last journey he would ever make. Dawn broke on Sunday 5 April, Easter Day, through a blinding snow storm, but land was sighted faintly ahead.

It was Holy Island. Captain and crew steered the vessel as best they could towards the narrow harbour. As they entered broadside, Ross saw the waves rise and part, like two great whales, and then close again behind them. Now, in the harbour, they were safe. A ship from Yarmouth, following not far behind them, could not make an entrance through the wall of water, and had to cast anchor. Ross was later to discover that she had broken up in the night and all life was lost.

Meanwhile, he and the crew were taken to the castle and offered hospitality by Captain Rugg, the governor of the Island. The next morning, Easter Monday, the islanders gathered on the shore to search the wreckage cast up by the storm. A box of fur hats with gold hatbands aroused the interest of two men – a certain gentleman, and a minister of the parish, a Scotsman named Lindsay. So determined were each to have them that they drew swords and fought furiously. Ross watched in fascination as an islander, taking advantage of the fracas, nipped in smartly and made off with the hats!

Ross spent one more night in the castle with Captain Rugg and the ship's crew and recorded that the castle 'had no strength at all'. He also noted Rugg's great nose, describing the Captain as 'a notable good fellow, as his great red nose full of pimples did give testimony'.

By Tuesday morning the storm had so far abated that the company were able to move on to an inn, where Captain Rugg told them many amusing tales. Eventually they set sail for Leith, and arrived there, as far as is known, without mishap. What Captain Rugg failed to realize is that he, a captain in the Protestant army, had given refuge to a Jesuit priest and helped him on his way. This entire story was told by Blakhal in an account of his travels written between 1631 and 1649, with the wonderful title 'A brieffe narration of the services done to three noble ladyes'!

In this account Blakhal reveals what Captain Rugg told him of the islanders' attitude towards ships that were endangered at sea:

> He was a very civil and jovial gentleman, and good company; and among the rest of his merry discourses, he tould [told] us how the common people ther [there] do pray for shippes which they sie [see] in danger. They al sit down on their knees, and hold up their handes, and say very devotedly, Lord send her to us, God send her to us. You, said he, seing them on their knees, and their hands joined, do think that they are praying for your sauvetie [safety]; but their myndes [minds] are far from that. They pray, not God to sauve [save] you, or send you to the port, but to send you to them by shipwreck, that they may gette the spoile of her. And to show that this is their meaning, said he, if the shippe come wel to the porte, or eschew [avoid] naufrage [ruin], they gette up in anger, crying the Devil stick her, she is away from us.

This is the sort of tale that was commonly told of communities along the coasts of England, but the truth is that folk risked their lives to save others. Wreckage on the beach was a different matter though: then it always seemed to be 'finders keepers'.

A century or so before Mr Blakhal's visit, the dissolution of the priory had not only led to the island people losing their main employer and protector, the Benedictines, but had also presented Henry VIII with a problem. Having earlier invaded France, he was well aware of the possibility that the French might stage a return invasion using Scotland as a back door, relations between Scotland and England at this stage being more than a little strained. And so in 1539 an Order of Council was issued saying that 'all Havens [harbours] should be fensed with bulwarks and blockehouses [forts] against the Scots'.

The first attempt at fortifying Holy Island harbour was in 1542 when the king ordered the Earl of Rutland to send workmen from Berwick. These included Robert Rooke, who planned to use the stone from the priory to build two bulwarks, one to defend the island and one to guard the sea road. He wrote:

> There is stone plentie [plenty] and sufficient remayning [remaining] of the olde abbey lately dissolved there to mak [make] the bulwark that shal defend the eland [island] all of stone if it maie [may] so stand with the good pleasure of the kinges [king's] said majestie [majesty].

It would appear that some building work done on Beblow Crag was completed by 1550 when Sir Robert Bowes wrote in 'A book of the state of the Frontiers and Marches between England and Scotland':

> The Fort Beblowe, within Holy Island, lyeth [lies] very well for the defence of the haven theire [there]; and if there were about the lower part thereof made a ring, with bulwarkes to flancke [flank] the same, the ditch [moat] thereabout might be easily watered towarde the land. And then I thinke the said forte were very stronge, and stood to a great purpose. Both for the defense of the forte and the annoyance of the enemies, if they did arrive in any other parte of island.

The moat was never created, and in fact it appears not much of the fort was built to any standard, for when Sir Richard Lee came on his inspection of northern defences in 1565 he noted: 'Biblawe . . . ys [is] nothinge but high rock and a platform made on the top and a vamure [false wall] theirof being of turf which is now consumed away.'

The Bowes report tells us of the poor state of the priory church, now being used as a naval storehouse:

> A piece also of the roofe of the great storehowse that was the Churche of the Priory, was the last yeare, in a great winde, broken downe by a parcel [section] of the imbattlement [parapet] of the same howse . . . which would [should] be repaired with expedicion [expediency], or ells [else] the weat [weight] discending [falling] therby [thereabouts] will cawse [cause] great decaye in the floores of the said storehowses.

Elizabeth I, mindful of the importance of Holy Island in the battle against the Scots, had engineers sent to the island in 1570. Sir William Reed, the then captain of the castle, saw to the building of 12-foot high walls on Beblow at the cost of £500. By 1572, under his supervision, the castle's basic shape as we know it, with its upper and lower batteries, was completed. The castle was now defended by proper artillery – culverins (large long-barrelled cannons), demi-culverins, plus light ship's cannons known as sakers and falcons. The garrison was made up of a captain, two master gunners (who earned 1 shilling a day), one master's mate (10d a day) and 20 soldiers (8d each). For the first time it seemed the castle would be useful in defence, but as it turned out, it would never be tested. With the Union of the Crowns under James I in 1603, the war with Scotland ended, though during the reign of Charles I – due to the religious antagonism between him and his Scottish subjects – the fort was repaired and improved in case of trouble.

Visitors to the island were impressed with the castle. Captain Rugg's hospitality and large red nose were often commented on. In 1635 the General of the Parliamentary forces in the Civil War, Sir William Brereton, wrote:

> In a dainty little fort there lives Captain Rugg, governor of the fort, who is famous for his generous free entertainment of strangers, as for his bottle nose which is the largest I have seen. There are neat warm rooms in the little fort.

In 1639 Charles I came north. Twenty ships under the command of the Marquis of Hamilton anchored below the castle and landed two regiments of foot soldiers. John Aston, a gentleman from Cheshire and one of the king's men, noted at this time that there were 24 men and a captain manning the castle, and that the soldiers were now only getting 6d per day. He also wrote: 'The captain at our being there was a Captain Rugg, known commonly for his great nose.'

Rugg had shown liberal hospitality to Parliamentarians and to Royalists as well as to Father Gilbert Blakhal the Jesuit. How

he managed this is hard to tell, for it seemed he was rarely paid
and that he owed many bills. In desperation, when the Royal
Paymasters were 16 months in arrears with his pay, he wrote
them a rhyming letter. It is dated 1643:

> The great Commander of the Gormorants,
> The Geese and Ganders of these Hallowed Lands,
> Where Lindisfarne and Holy Iland [Island] stands,
> These worthless lines sends to yo' [your] worthie hands . . .
> Send in my disbursements [salary], made out by direction
>   [on the orders]
> From my good lord [the king]; sirs, hasten my collection
>   [payment] . . .
> I owe for bread, beere and beefe in sundry places;
> The cuntrie [country] calls upon [showers] me with disgraces
>   [disapproval] . . .
> I wish I had wherewith for to inter me [enough to live on];
> Thus to yor [your] best discressions [mercy] I refer me,
> And that greate God that houlds [keeps] the Devil in fetters,
> Blesse good Kinge Charles, myselfe and you my debters.

Poor Rugg never did receive his pay. He died in 1646 and in his
will left a legacy of £100, owed to him by Parliament, to his
daughter. The garrison appear not to have received any of the
monies due until ten years later and then only after litigation by
the widow of the governor who followed Rugg.

By 1715, the time of the first Jacobite Rising in Scotland,
when supporters of James VII of Scotland and II of England,
who had been deposed by Parliament, attempted to return him
to the throne, there was a sergeant, a corporal and ten or twelve
men at the castle. On 10 October, a Northumbrian gentleman
by the name of Lancelot Errington anchored his brigantine in
the harbour and invited all who were not on duty at the castle
to come on board and have some brandy. Soon his guests
had consumed enough to make them all quite incapable. Then
on some pretence, Lancelot and his nephew Mark Errington
returned armed to the castle. They knocked out the sentinel,
ejected an old gunner, the corporal and two soldiers, then shut

the gates, hoisted the Pretender's (James VII's) flag and claimed the castle for the Jacobite cause. For two nights they were able to enjoy the glory.

On the third day, however, soldiers arrived from Berwick. Lancelot and Mark tried to escape but Lancelot was wounded by a bullet, and both were taken prisoner. Later they managed to burrow out of the prison in Berwick, hide at Bamburgh for nine days, then escape to France. When the Jacobite cause had been suppressed, the two took advantage of a general pardon to return to Newcastle. It is said Lancelot died of a broken heart after hearing news of the disastrous battle of Culloden in 1746, from which 'Bonnie Prince Charlie', grandson of James II, was forced to flee into exile.

The castle saw little activity from then on. In the nineteenth century it was manned by a Voluntary Coast Artillery which finally left in 1893. Later coastguards used it as a rough barracks, and it was allowed to fall into a very poor, almost ruinous state.

———•◆•———

In 1901 Edward Hudson, founder of *Country Life* magazine, came across the castle while on holiday. Having scaled its walls, he looked with some delight on its neglected and disordered interior – strewn with broken furniture and crockery as it was – for as a great romantic, he saw the castle's possibilities. Having decided to amuse himself with the place, he leased it from the Crown and invited the leading architect of the day to the island with the words, 'Have got Lindisfarne'.

That architect was Edwin Lutyens, who had been introduced to Hudson by the influential garden designer Gertrude Jekyll in 1899. Lutyens had worked on Jekyll's house at Munstead Wood in Surrey, and had been commissioned to design Hudson's country house, Deanery Garden, in Sonning, Berkshire. The three had become friends, and nothing could have been more natural than for Hudson to invite Lutyens, a master of the Tudor Revival style, to create a summer holiday home for him in the shell of what had originally been a Tudor fort.

Though outwardly remaining much the same, Lutyens' removal of the castle's crenellations (or ramparts) gave it a simpler, more fluid silhouette, and made it appear like a sea bird nesting on the rock. The approach to the castle was made more dramatic by the removal of the protecting stone balustrade and the placing of cobbles in Lutyens' signature herring-bone pattern on the shallow stepped ramp. Interestingly, when the Prince and Princess of Wales (the future King George V and Queen Mary) visited in 1908, the lack of protection of a wall by the ramp worried the Prince, and the Princess complained that the cobbles hurt her feet!

Lutyens loved dramatic entrances and passage ways, and his entrance hall to the castle reflects something of the style of the old priory or even the Norman nave of Durham Cathedral in having rounded pillars and 'Norman' arches. You have a feeling of entering a church, and indeed if you ignored its fine furnishings and saw the castle only by candlelight, it would have had quite a monastic feel to it. The dining room and ship room with their old vaulted ceilings – designed to take the weight of the cannons on the battery above – have undecorated stone walls, and the floors throughout are of herring-bone-patterned brick or flag stone. The castle could hardly ever have been warm even if it was only designed for summer occupation.

The austere floors, walls and ceilings are in fact wonderfully offset by the honey-coloured oak of the doors, with their splendid lead-weighted latches, and the mainly Tudor furnishings. Lutyens designed the oval table in the dining room, the long table and the little wall cupboards in the east bedroom, and the dresser and refectory table in the kitchen. There is a good deal of English and Flemish oak furniture from the seventeenth century, and the dining room and kitchen have some lovely copper work by the pioneering arts and crafts designer W. A. S. Benson. The overall effect is reminiscent of a Vermeer painting, especially when the soft light comes in through the windows, and in fact photographs of the Lutyens children in the castle recall the Dutch seventeenth-century interiors so loved by their father and Hudson.

It might be suggested that beauty and balance have been achieved somewhat at the expense of comfort, but when Hudson was in residence the castle received many special visitors. The Prince and Princess of Wales drove across the sands with a retinue of eight carriages; Prime Minister Herbert Asquith came with his daughter Lady Violet Bonham Carter; the conductor Sir Malcolm Sargent, the author of *Peter Pan* J. M. Barrie, and the ballerina Alicia Markova all visited at various times. Lytton Strachey, the historian, was one of the few who complained about the cold and lack of comfort, while one of Hudson's favourite visitors was the famous cellist Madame Guilhermina Suggia. He had her portrait painted by Augustus John (the magnificent oil was later presented to the Tate Gallery) and gave her a Stradivarius as a present. The island often buzzed with rumours of who was staying at the castle.

Gertrude Jekyll was invited to come and design the castle's small walled garden – originally used by the garrison to grow its vegetables – which lay about a third of a mile to the north. The walls were rebuilt and inner paving laid in the spring of 1911. The aim was to produce a garden of flowers that would be at its best in the summer when Hudson was in residence.

In 2003 we celebrated the 150th anniversary of Gertrude Jekyll's birth – the garden having been re-created according to her original plan by the National Trust and a sundial placed there – and I was reminded of a story told to me by an old retired fisherman.

One day in 1906, Lutyens met Gertrude Jekyll at Kings Cross railway station for the journey to Lindisfarne. Miss Jekyll's luggage included a portfolio for her paintings, a three-legged stool and 3 shillings' (15 pence) worth of bullseye sweets to suck, while Lutyens had two Gladstone bags, one containing a live raven called 'Black Jack'. They travelled as far as Belford by train, and were then transported across the countryside to Ross

Links where a fishing boat waited to row them to the castle. On arrival, Lutyens, a slight man, was easily carried across the last stretch of shallow water by a fisherman, who then returned for Miss Jekyll. However, here his attempts proved quite inadequate. Rumour has it that he had to enlist the help of three more sturdy islanders before Miss Jekyll could be brought safely to shore.

Once installed in the castle, that redoubtable woman set about creating a walled garden in the garrison's old vegetable plot. She also wanted the castle crag itself planted with flowers, and devised an ingenious method of doing so. A small boy (in fact the uncle of my narrator) was put into one basket, flowers into another, and both lowered from the castle window. The 'old lady gardener', as she soon became known, pointed with her stick from the ship-room window. Wherever she pointed, the boy planted. Islanders used to come out and watch this wonderful sight.

It was not until 1918 that Hudson got the freehold of the castle. In 1921, he sold it for £11,000 to Oswald 'Foxy' Falk who after a few years sold it on to Sir Edward de Stein. He used it as his summer holiday home, and though he gave the castle to the National Trust in 1944, remained as its tenant until 1965.

Early one summer's morning I went down to the harbour. There was a low mist over the sea and the neighbouring fields, but the castle rose majestically through the cloud. No wonder it is one of the great icons of Northumberland, often seen as a place of romance. In a moment, I was caught up in the story of William of Middleton.

One of William's ancestors was the prior of Holy Island. William himself lived just opposite the island on the mainland, and had two great loves: Rupert, his fine horse, and Annie, the daughter of Romero, who was in charge of the troops on Holy Island. William had to meet with Annie secretly, as he and her father were at war with each other. A ballad from the nine-teenth century tells how he came over from the mainland:

> He cantered o'er the Fenham Flatts,
> When the tide was back awhile
> Which once a day changes that spot
> From continent to isle.

William rode to the east shore and stabled his horse in a cave. From the castle Annie had been on the lookout, and met him on the eastern shore. But someone saw the couple together and told her father, who flew into a rage. The year before, William had killed Romero's nephew in a battle, and Romero swore he would now be revenged by hanging William and putting Annie in the priory dungeon. He decided, 'I will wait until the tide is in and then we will catch them with no way of escape.' When the time came, Romero and a henchman challenged William to fight. William now had a difficult decision to make, for what would Annie think if he killed her father? As the hench-man drew his sword, William drew his and managed quickly to dispatch the enemy. Then he sharply turned, caught Romero off guard and knocked him out. Before he came to, Annie and William had mounted Rupert and begun making for the tide-covered Flatts. Romero stormed off and promised a purse of gold to any boat that could capture them, and soon four fisher-men were in pursuit of the horse nobly swimming in the sea. Three times Annie was almost washed off by the waves, and three times William held her fast.

> The steed it swam, the coble [boat] shot [moved at speed]
> Whilst fisher's raxed [pounded] the oars
> Was there such a race, the steed I say
> Fist [first] landed on Fenham shore.

They had escaped. Soon they were wed and in a year had a lovely son. There the tale should end like all good folk tales but it does not. When William was riding down Chesterhill (where I live now), he met an old woman who told him to beware for his horse would kill him. William could not believe it and tried to forget what he was told. But in the next few days, for no apparent reason, the horse threw him twice. William now became worried: he dare not risk the prophecy, so regretfully he took Rupert down to the sandy Flatts, drew his sword and killed him there. The tide would take him away. Again now the story should end but it does not. A few months later William had a visitor and took him down to the Flatts to look out towards Holy Island and enjoy a walk. As they strolled William saw a stone shining in the sand and gave it a hard kick. The stone shattered for it was the skull of his horse. A piece of bone pierced through his boot and into his foot. Almost immediately poison began to set in. When William got home a doctor was called but nothing could be done. Rupert had killed his master. Like many ballads this is a sad story, but happily it has no ending, for it is said that on a moonlit night when the tide is in and the white waves are gleaming, you can look towards the mainland from Holy Island and see William and Annie riding Rupert in the sea. From the vantage point of the vicarage I had the best chance to look over the waves on many a moonlit night.

Both God and the Devil

'How shall I like this place? It is cut off from the world.'
There was an odd note of scorn in the little man's voice as
he answered. 'It is the world, sir. Here within these hills, in this
space of ground, is all the world . . . in every village through
which I have passed since then I have found the whole world –
all anger and vanity and covetousness and lust, yes, and all
charity, goodness and sweetness of soul. But most of all here
in this valley, I have found the whole world . . . You will find
everything here, sir. God and the devil both walk in these
fields.'   (Hugh Walpole, *Rogue Herries*, London, 1930)

A friend was horrified when I told him I was going to become
the vicar of Holy Island. 'Why do you want to cut yourself off
from the world?' he asked. Seven months later he came for a
visit on an ordinary day in August: I took six services, over five
hundred people passed through the church, and I counselled
many more that were in need or looking for guidance. All
my friend could say was, 'You're right in the thick of it here.'
The quote at the beginning of this chapter came to mind.
Holy Island is a special place, a holy place, but it is also an ordinary place with all the joys and sorrows, all the troubles and
triumphs of any community.

Bede tells us how Cuthbert often did not sleep but walked
around the island to see how things were. Walking around the
island is one of my delights in any season or weather. I love
to stand out at Castle Point when the wind is raging and the
sea is rough. Mighty waves come towards you with great force,
expressing the huge energies that have broken on this little
island. It is hard for the summer visitor to appreciate the effect
these have had on the heart and soul of islanders down through
the centuries, for it takes time and sensitivity to appreciate the

way Lindisfarne has responded to the many factors that have shaped it.

We know that the island was at a low ebb after the dissolution of the priory, with people struggling to make a living, and it would seem that little had improved by the time of the English Civil War (1642–51), when the island suffered at the hands of both the Parliamentarians and their enemies, the Royalists. By 1721, Holy Island is described thus:

> The town of Holy Island is an ancient town, and the inhabitants are distinguished into burgesses as they are called in ancient writings, or freemen and stallengers. The burgesses or freemen are those who have houses in the town called freehold houses in number 24. The stallengers are the owners of other houses. There are belonging to the freehold houses certain lands inclosed as there are crofts and gardens belonging to the stallengers houses. The rest of the island (save the lord's pasture close) is sandy soil whereon grows a sort of grass called bents, and is common among the freemen, who each have a right to depasture a certain number of cattle thereon, and to cut the bents for covering their houses, to dig in the freestone quarries for stone for their use, to keep a fishing boat for the catching of cod and other fish, to cure and dry them on the common field, where there is a place made for the purpose, and to draw their boats for safety above the full sea mark, and lay them on the said common. The stallengers have a right to depasture their cattle also but are stinted to a lesser number than the freemen are.
>
> (James Raine, *North Durham*, Part 1, London, J. B. Nichols & Son, 1830, p. 161)

After the Enclosure Act of 1793 the potential for farming was better developed. The freemen gave up their right of common ground and were granted in return small plots of land near the village. The areas of Popplewell, Jenny Bell's Well and the Brigwell were declared for public use as they provided the islanders with a water supply. The fishermen were still allowed to use the harbour area for their trade though it was put into the hands of the lord of the manor. Land was set aside for a workhouse and a school. In 1796, through public subscription, a National School and an adjoining teacher's house was built on land that had been set aside under the Enclosure Act. The population at this point was about 350 people.

William Hutchinson, writing in his 'The History and Antiquities of the County Palatine of Durham' in 1794, saw the potential of the natural reserves of the island and observed that life was beginning to improve:

> The village consists of a few irregular houses; two or more of which are inns, one appertains to a farm-hold, and the rest are inhabited by fishermen. It has been improved of late years by the building of a few tenements . . .
>
> The fishermen in the winter season, are employed in catching lobsters, which are sent in great quantities to the London market. Ten or twelve, three or four-men boats are used in the summer, fishing for cod, ling haddocks, which abound on the coast.

Hutchinson notes:

> On the north part of the island, there is abundance of limestone; and a small seam of coal, never much worked, on account of the water and other difficulties. There is plenty of iron ore in a bed of black shiver or slate . . . The Carron company have men getting iron ore, but they are obliged to work at the ebbing of the tide, as the ore lies within the water mark.

The Carron Iron Company was based near Falkirk on the Firth of Forth and was one of the major iron producers in the British Isles. It gave its name to a light cannon which was used by Nelson's navy and called the carronade. However, the amount of iron nodules it could collect on Holy Island was very small, and extraction soon proved unsustainable.

We get a jaundiced glimpse of island life from a young man named William Ferguson, who moved to Lindisfarne from Eyemouth, a fishing town north of Berwick, at the age of 12.

A few years later, in 1782, he tells of the lawlessness of Holy Island, but as this account is part of his 'conversion' statement to Methodism it is probably best treated with some reserve:

> The people of this place were mostly smugglers, and the children remarkedy wicked! Of these I soon learnt to curse and swear, and to glory in my shame. I learned to tell lies for sport, to play at cards, to dance, to work the greatest part of the Sabbath Day: and to make a mock of all religious people, saying they were all hypocrites. And this deplorable condition I remained till I was near 20 years old.
>
> So I continued fast asleep in the devil's arms, till one day I was working in the shop with my father, my mind ran upon a match of drinking and dancing in which I was engaged to join in the evening. Suddenly I hear a voice from heaven saying, 'What if thou shouldest drop down dead in the midst of the dance! Wouldest thou go to heaven?'
>
> I said, 'No I am not fit for heaven.'
>
> I immediately felt I had passed sentence upon myself; and if I went not to heaven hell was my portion; light broke in: I was filled with horror: I saw myself hanging over the mouth of hell, by the little thread of life.
>
> In the evening my company came in to carry me to dancing. To their surprise they found me reading the Bible.
>
> They asked my father and mother, 'Are you not willing he should go with us?'
>
> They said, 'Yes, but we think he is not well.'
>
> They said, 'Come we shall soon cure him.'
>
> 'Do', said another, 'and I will carry his fiddle.'
>
> I looked at them all very mildly, 'If you do carry me, I shall be of no use to you. For a dance I will not dance this night: and a tune I will not play.'
>
> They stared and left me.
>
> As soon as the inhabitants of the Island found I would not drink, swear or work on the Lord's Day, they were violently angry, so that I could hardly walk the street, for a mob setting upon me. And my father and mother insisted that I worked on the Lord's Day. But I told them, 'No, never more: I will sooner have the flesh torn off my bones.'

Here we see the island as it is, an ordinary working place, where people enjoy a night out, drink, play cards and organize their own music and dancing. We also perceive that some religious-minded people want to observe a different way of life. These tensions have existed on the island for a good few centuries, though most people have become more tolerant of late.

Another view of the island, in which we should be aware of some class distinction and snobbery at work, is that of a gentleman from a nearby village on the mainland. In his 'Our visit to Holy Island in May 1854', Dr George Johnston of Ilderton writes:

> Our stroll through the village disclosed very sensibly the nature of the principal occupation of the natives. In every street heaps of the shells of the mussel and limpet are collected before the doors, and mixed with the refuse of fishing lines and with the household ashes, etc. They do send forth a most foul and fishy smell, evidently agreeable to the senses of the householders. Men, and more women, were sitting in the sun at the doors, occupied in baiting the lines for the morrow . . .
>
> A number of skates were laid on the tiled roofs of many of the houses, to be dried by the sun. They were not ornamental, and sent forth a pungent smell. When fully dried they become a favourite relish to the fishermen when drinking their ale; and I was told they were much in demand by the sailors of the Scotch vessels that are driven here for shelter. They are eaten without preparation or simply toasted at the fire.

Dr Johnson also gives us a depressing picture of St Mary's church:

> The Church is cold, damp and musty within; the walls covered with green mould, and 'sclaters' (wood lice) were crawling on the paved floor. The seats were unfitted for the service, so much so that neither male nor female can kneel on any part of it. Every seat has a large brass plate on the door, engraved with the name of its proprietor: and the 'Border Brewery' has three seats to its share. The conduct of the service suited the Church; there

were no responses made, and a very considerable proportion of the small flock had no books. Enough!

Not a pretty picture of the island but one common to most fishing communities. An offering of dried skate and ale would not have been to everyone's taste!

Another writer called Walter White, who was hiking around Britain, gives us his impressions of the 'town and the boats setting off on an evening tide' in his book *Northumberland and the Border* (1859):

> There is a square bestrewn with unsavoury rubbish, and the condition of the streets accords therewith, implying that public cleanliness has not yet grown into a habit. The spring is a good way off. Whitewashed cottages, some of them retaining the primitive thatch, constituted the bulk of the dwellings, while among those of better style appear nine inns or public-houses (The Ship Inn, The Fishermen's arms, The Selby Arms, The Northumberland Arms, The Castle Hotel, The Britannia, The Plough Inn, The Crown and Anchor, and the Iron Rails). In the last census returns the population of the island is given as 908, of whom 458 are males; hence, excluding boys, we may form a notion as to the number of customers to each public house. It is said that if good lodgings were available, the island would be more visited than it is by sea-bathers; but the difficulty of access and the want of pleasant scenery are perhaps the chief reasons against immigration.

I wonder what this writer would think if he saw the flow of the half a million visitors a year to the island. White continues:

> We saw the 'town' under its busy aspect, preparing for the herring fishery; nets lay in heaps, or stretched out fifty or sixty yards, while men and boys disentangle their mazy folds and tie loops; around almost every door lies a heap of floats, and lines and queer looking oilskin garments, and ample sou'westers hanging on the walls. And at times a few men, wearing sea-going jackets, and boots up to their hips, take their way down to the beach with a pile of gear on their shoulders. They will sail ere long, for rumour says the herring are in the offing . . .

We passed the beach where the fishing boats come in, and saw the huge wooden vat – if vat it be – round which women stand to clean the herrings, and on the other side of the road fourteen hundred herring-barrels in piles and rows, and two men industrious over their preparation. 'There wouldn't be any too many', they said, 'not yet half enough, if the boats did have but luck' . . .

While crossing the herring beach, we had a pretty sight in the departure of a number of boats. The tide served, evening was coming on, and one after another they hoisted sail, stood out of the bay, made tack, some two tacks, and then away to the open sea, perhaps for five and twenty miles.

There are images of the island women carrying water from the wells and rushing with tubs to catch rain water from the projecting spouts of the church. While the tubs were filling (and they would not be very light to carry full) the women would busy themselves seeking out docken leaves on which to lay fishing hooks to bait. Baiting the lines day after day with lugworm left them with sore fingers. Of course, they would still have all the household work and cooking to do.

The second half of the nineteenth century saw the island at its busiest, both at sea, with great catches of herring, and on the land. As part of the Industrial Revolution its earlier involvement in lime-burning was developed, with five ships continually carrying lime to Dundee and bringing back coal for the burning process. The light from kiln fires could be seen on the mainland and far out to sea, and it was at this time that the two strange pinnacles on Ross Sands were constructed to guide the ships safely into harbour.

A story from around this time shows Holy Island village rather like a frontier town. The crew of the coble, the *Ready Made Easy*, which comprised four characters named Nodding Jimmy, Barber Wull, Tom the Dregger and Bassie Gull, met regularly in the Fishermen's Arms. This is now a private residence known as Town View and looks down Marygate – I have been there many a time, and it would have made a very small drinking house! Nonetheless, here in front of the bar-kitchen the crew would share out the earnings from their catch for the week, and see who could drink the most beer without having to leave their seat. The winner of this contest was excused from paying for drinks on the two following Fridays. The landlord, Ritchie Gardiner, was a good friend, but he often got tired long before the drinking had ended. One Saturday morning, when the fire had burned low, he snuffed out the candles, but the fishermen failed to take the hint and did not budge. Deciding this called for stronger measures, Ritchie went behind the bar, brought out a pistol and threatened to shoot them. They left for home! If they had looked a little closer they would have realized that the 'pistol' was a black pudding in the shape of a sausage. The island enjoyed a good laugh and the fishermen involved often told this story against themselves.

One yarn, still repeated today to anyone foolhardy enough to believe it, concerns using crabs instead of ferrets to flush rabbits out from the Coney Warren at the Snook. A strong large dog-crab, with a piece of burning tallow candle about an inch long stuck on its back, is sent down a rabbit hole. Rabbits bolt out into a net, as if confronted by a ferret! Anyone with sense knows the crab would not go in and the candle would soon go out, but this tale is in many books about Holy Island.

With so many fishermen, it is natural that those on the island should be involved in rescuing those in peril on the sea, and in response to Captain Rugg's suggestion that they encouraged the wrecking of ships, it has to be said that island homes have always been ready to offer hospitality, food and warmth to those in need of shelter. Many lives have been saved since the first island lifeboat came into use in 1786, though the service has not always been restricted to rescue at sea. In the severe winter of 1947, when all local roads were blocked with deep snow and the island was running out of provisions, the lifeboat was dispatched to Berwick for supplies. On its return journey, it also brought back the body of an islander whose funeral had been arranged for the next day.

It was an emotional time in March 1968 when the last life-boat station on the island was finally closed. For almost two hundred years, local men had risked their lives for their fellow men, and there were many tales of valour and of great heroism. But the ships of today are able to withstand dangers that would have overpowered the vessels of the past. Seahouses lifeboat station in the south and Berwick station in the north now protect the coast, in conjunction with the Sea King helicopter at RAF Boulmer, though the latter spends more time rescuing stranded motorists from the Causeway than people from the sea.

Today, the 'hunter-gatherer' way of life the islanders have maintained for thousands of years struggles to survive. The number of fishermen and boats is greatly diminished, and the income of those who do fish is often augmented by the money their wives bring in by going out to work or running a bed and breakfast. Fishing policies, safety regulations, insurance premiums, foreign fishing vessels and the cost of boats and diesel have contributed to the loss as much as diminishing stocks of fish.

However, there is a thriving winery on the island selling 'Lindisfarne Mead' and many other products. A family from off the island are farming 'Lindisfarne Oysters' from the tidal flats. It is possible that with some assistance, the fishermen or others could develop the mussel-bed near Black Law, and if a small processing plant were built, this would provide yet another home-grown industry. The Heritage Centre, the National Trust and English Heritage all provide employment on the island. The Holy Island Development Trust, who own the Heritage Centre, has successfully provided some affordable housing for rent to keep young folk on the island, and is in the process of building more homes. The village hall has been demolished and the way is being prepared for the building of a new one. Due to computers, more can be done from home, and some islanders are venturing into selling their goods online. When one was asked if he worried about global warming, he replied, 'We are higher above the sea than many a place including great parts of London. We are used to being an island where a lot of coast communities are not. Why worry too much!' The future seems far brighter for the island community than many communities of the same size.

Amid much change, the islanders try to hold on to some of their traditions. On the first day of the New Year, the men form small groups and seek to visit every house on the island. They bring a drink with them, are given a drink by their host, and sometimes find they need a bit of a rest before continuing on their rounds! On the second day of the year, the women of the island have their turn, decked in tinsel and baubles to bring some sparkle to the dark days of early January.

At the end of the wildfowling season the local gunners have a 'Duck Supper' – a 'men only' affair, in which everyone has a whole duck on his plate plus vegetables and potatoes from the island. It's an event which can go on well into the early hours of the next morning.

Weddings on the island are wonderfully joyous occasions. When the bride and groom leave the church and draw near to the priory, the bride has to jump the 'petting stone', which is the base of an old high standing cross. She is assisted by two of the oldest men on the island and it is considered good luck if she makes the jump in one go. When the couple come to the church gates, they find the gates have been tied with rope and have to pay a 'toll' for it to be undone. Then they have to face a fusillade of guns, as wildfowlers and fishermen discharge cartridge after cartridge causing a great din and much smoke. This has something to do with chasing away evil, but looks like a scene from a Wild West film (and makes every marriage a 'shotgun wedding'!). Next, coins are scattered in Market Place for the children to collect. Finally, before the happy couple go off to their reception, the bride kneels down and has a napkin placed on her head. Then a plate with a piece of cake, made from the same mixture as the wedding cake, is thrown over her head. It is good luck (and symbolic!) for the plate to break.

In the vicarage late one afternoon, I prepared for the daily evening service. It was a dark stormy night and we would be lighting a candle at the beginning of the service to show how the light is stronger than the darkness. Later, we would close the day with a prayer that is used in quite a few island homes and pinned in at least two of its fishing boats:

Bless, O Lord, this Island,
This Holy Island,
Make it a place of peace and prosperity,
Make it a place of light and love,
Make it a place of holiness and hospitality,
Make it a place of grace and generosity,
And begin with me.

Timeline

Many dates in the early part of this period are uncertain. The following is an approximate guide.

547–93   Ida comes to Bamburgh and rules Bernicia.

c. 590   Urien, a Christian king, murdered at the siege of Inis Metcaud (early name for Holy Island).

593   Aethelfrith succeeds to Bernicia.

597   Augustine's mission arrives at Canterbury.

603   Aethelfrith marries Acha of Deira. This marriage brings about the union of Bernicia and Deira into the kingdom of Northumbria. British church refuses to help Augustine's mission.

616   Aethelfrith's victory at Chester; he kills monks at prayer. Edwin defeats Aethelfrith and becomes king of all Northumbria.
Aethelfrith's children, Eanfrith, Oswald, Oswy and Ebba, go into exile at Iona and the kingdom of Dalriada.

625   Edwin marries Ethelburga, a Christian princess from Kent. She brings Paulinus as her chaplain.
Baptism of Edwin's daughter Eanfled.

627   Baptism of Edwin and Hilda at York by Paulinus.
Conversion of Northumbria by Paulinus.

628   Birth of Benedict Biscop.

632   Edwin killed by Penda at Hatfield Chase.
Paulinus and Queen Ethelburga flee the kingdom.
Eanfrith and Osric seek to take over Bernicia and Deira.

633   Eanfrith and Osric are killed.

634   Oswald defeats Penda and kills Cadwallon at the battle of Heavenfield on Hadrian's Wall near Hexham.

Oswald invites a mission from Iona to Northumbria. Corman arrives but soon returns to Iona.

635 Aidan comes to Northumbria at Oswald's invitation and establishes a monastery on Lindisfarne.

642 Oswald killed by Penda at Oswestry.
Oswy succeeds to Bernicia and Oswin to Deira. Both continue to support the Lindisfarne mission.

643 Oswy marries Eanfled in an attempt to unite the two kingdoms.

c. 650 Penda attacks Bamburgh.

651 Oswin is assassinated on the instructions of Oswy.
Aidan dies at Bamburgh on 31 August and is buried on Lindisfarne.
Cuthbert has a vision of angels taking Aidan to heaven. He enters the monastery at Melrose.
Finan becomes the bishop of Lindisfarne.

653 Wilfrid and Benedict Biscop set out for Lyon and Rome.
Paeda, son of Penda, baptized.

657 Hilda becomes abbess of Whitby.

661 Finan dies. Colman made bishop of Lindisfarne.

664 The Synod of Whitby.
Tuda, who succeeded Colman, dies of the plague and is replaced by Eata.
Cuthbert is invited to become the prior of Lindisfarne.

668 Theodore of Tarsus consecrated as Archbishop of Canterbury.

673 Birth of Bede.

676 Cuthbert is given permission to become a hermit on Inner Farne.

685 Cuthbert is made bishop of Lindisfarne at York.

687 Cuthbert retires as bishop and returns to Inner Farne where he dies.

698 Cuthbert's body elevated and found intact.
Lindisfarne Gospels created before 720.

Timeline

793	Viking invasion of Lindisfarne.
875	Monks leave Lindisfarne with the body of Cuthbert and Lindisfarne Gospels.
1069	Cuthbert's body brought back for the winter.
1093	Work begins on building the Benedictine priory.
1537	Dissolution of the monasteries including Lindisfarne.
1572	Castle completed on Beblow Crag.
1902	Edward Hudson buys the castle and employs Edward Lutyens and Gertrude Jekyll.
1944	Castle given to the National Trust.

Glossary

Adda   seventh-century priest on Lindisfarne

Aethelfrith   ferocious sixth/seventh-century king of Northumbria, father of *Oswald*, *Oswy*

Aethelred   eighth-century king of Northumbria

Aldfrith   seventh-century king of Northumbria, son of *Oswy* and *Fina*, half-brother of *Alchfrith*

Agatho   seventh-century priest

Agilbert   seventh-century Frankish bishop of Wessex and Paris

Aidan   seventh-century abbot of Lindisfarne, bishop of Northumbria

Alchfled   seventh-century queen of south Mercia (English kingdom in the Midlands), daughter of *Oswy*

Alchfrith   seventh-century sub-king of Deira (southern Northumbrian kingdom), son of *Oswy* and *Rhianmelt*, half-brother of *Aldfrith*

Alcuin   eighth-century master of Charlemagne's school

Aldfrith   seventh-century king of Northumbria, love child of *Oswy* and *Fina*, half-brother of *Alchfrith*

Aldred   tenth-century Northumbrian translator

Aneurin   seventh-century Welsh poet

Augustine   sixth/seventh-century missionary Archbishop of Canterbury

Bede, The Venerable   seventh/eighth-century monk of Jarrow, historian

Benedict Biscop   seventh-century abbot of Wearmouth and Jarrow, companion of *Wilfrid*

Betti   seventh-century priest on Lindisfarne

Billfrith   seventh/eighth-century Lindisfarne goldsmith

Boisil   seventh-century prior of Melrose Abbey

Cadwallon   seventh-century king of Gwynedd (in Wales)

Caelin   seventh-century chaplain to *Ethelwald*, brother of *Chad*, *Cedd* and *Cynibil*

Glossary

Cedd seventh-century bishop of Essex, abbot of Lastingham, brother of *Chad*, *Caelin* and *Cynibil*

Chad seventh-century bishop of York and Lichfield, brother of *Cedd*, *Caelin* and *Cynibil*

Charles I (1600–49), king of England, Scotland and Ireland

Colman seventh-century abbot of Lindisfarne, bishop of Northumbria

Corman seventh-century Iona monk

Cuthbert seventh-century bishop of Lindisfarne

Cynibil seventh-century monk, brother of *Chad*, *Cedd* and *Caelin*

Diuma seventh-century Irish bishop of Repton

Eadbert seventh-century bishop of Lindisfarne

Eadfrith seventh/eighth-century Lindisfarne scribe

Eanfled *Oswy*'s queen, daughter of *Edwin*, half-sister of *Egfrith*

Eardulph ninth-century last bishop of Lindisfarne and first bishop of Northumbria

Ebba seventh-century abbess of Coldingham

Ecgred ninth-century bishop of Lindisfarne

Edwin seventh-century king of Northumbria, father of *Egfrith*

Egfrith seventh-century king of Northumbria, son of *Edwin*, half-brother of *Eanfled*

Elizabeth I (1553–1603), queen of England and queen of Ireland

Ethelwald seventh/eighth-century bishop of Lindisfarne

Ethelwine eleventh-century, last Anglo-Saxon bishop of Durham

Fflamddwyn 'the flame bearer', sixth-century English foe of *Urien*

Fina seventh-century Irish princess, mother of *Aldfrith*, her love child with *Oswy*, sister of *Finan*

Finan seventh-century Irish abbot of Lindisfarne, bishop of Northumbria, brother of *Fina*

Gwallawg sixth-century ruler of the kingdom of Elmet (around Leeds)

Hadrian   seventh-century assistant to Bishop *Theodore*, not to be confused with the second-century Roman emperor who caused the Roman Wall to be built across Britain.

Harold II   (*c.* 1022–66) Anglo-Saxon king of England, killed at the Battle of Hastings by Norman invaders led by *William the Conqueror*

Heiu   seventh-century abbess of Hartlepool

Henry VIII   (1491–1547), king of England, later king of Ireland and claimant to the kingdom of France

Higbald   eighth/ninth-century bishop of Lindisfarne

Hilda   seventh-century abbess of Whitby

Hunwald   seventh-century friend of *Oswin*, whom he betrayed

Hussa   descendant of *Ida*

Ida   sixth-century king of Bernicia (northern Northumbrian kingdom)

James   seventh-century Roman deacon in Northumbria

James VI and I   (1566–1625), king of Scotland as James VI and king of England and king of Ireland as James I

Jerome   fourth/fifth-century Christian apologist, best known for translating the Vulgate, a popular Latin version of the Bible

Morcant   sixth-century king from the north of Britain, murderer of *Urien*

Oswald   seventh-century king of Northumbria, son of *Aethelfrith*, brother of *Oswy*

Oswin   seventh-century king of Deira (southern Northumbrian kingdom)

Oswy   sixth-century king of Bernicia (northern Northumbrian kingdom) and Northumbria, son of *Aethelfrith*, brother of *Oswald*

Owain   sixth-century British king of Rheged (around Solway Firth), son of *Urien*

Paulinus   seventh-century Roman bishop of York and Rochester

Peada   seventh-century sub-king of Mercia (English kingdom in the Midlands), son of *Penda*

Penda   seventh-century king of Mercia (English kingdom in the Midlands)

Reed, Sir William of Fenham   sixteenth/seventeenth-century governor of Lindisfarne castle

Reginald of Durham   twelfth-century monk at Durham, hagiologist

Rhianmelt   'Queen of Lightning', seventh-century princess of Rheged, great-granddaughter of *Urien*, *Oswy*'s queen (before *Eanfled*)

Rhydderch the Old   sixth-century king of Strathclyde (around Glasgow)

Romanus   seventh-century Roman chaplain to *Eanfled*

Ronan   seventh-century Irish monk

Rugg, Captain Robin   seventeenth-century governor of Lindisfarne castle

Segene   seventh-century abbot of Iona

Sigbert   seventh-century king of East Anglia

Simeon   eleventh/twelfth-century monk at Durham, English chronicler

Sparke, Thomas   sixteenth-century prior of Lindisfarne

Taliesin   sixth-century poet

Theodore (also **Theodore of Tarsus**)   seventh-century Greek Archbishop of Canterbury

Tondhere   seventh-century nobleman, assassinated with *Oswin*

Trumwine   seventh-century bishop of the Northumbrian see of the Picts

Tuda   seventh-century abbot of Lindisfarne and bishop of Northumbria

Urien   sixth-century king of British kingdom of Rheged (around Solway Firth), father of *Owain*, great-grandfather of *Rhianmelt*

Utta   seventh-century priest, *Oswy*'s chaplain

Wilfrid   seventh/eighth-century abbot of Ripon, bishop of York

Glossary

William of Calais   eleventh-century bishop of Durham
William the Conqueror (also **William I of England**)   (*c.* 1028–
   c. 1087), king of England after defeating *Harold II* at the Battle
   of Hastings in 1066